# The Land and People of
# GERMANY

GERMANY is a land of many contrasts, including within its boundaries such different sections as the wild, beautiful Bavarian Alps and the densely populated, heavily industrial Ruhr. Its position in the very heart of the continent has been a vital force in European affairs throughout history.

In this up-to-the-minute edition the authors tell of a new Germany which, despite its present state of flux and the uncertainties about its future, has forged ahead to become a leading nation in the world and the most prosperous in Europe.

# PORTRAITS OF THE NATIONS SERIES

*Also in the same format*

# The Land and People of
# GERMANY

by Raymond A. Wohlrabe
and Werner E. Krusch

REVISED EDITION 1972

PORTRAITS OF THE NATIONS SERIES

J. B. LIPPINCOTT COMPANY

Philadelphia          New York

The authors wish to thank the following for the use of photographs on the pages indicated: Deutschen Zentrale fuer Fremdenverkehr: 104, 136, Autenrieth Photo: 81, Diederichs Photo: 117, Henle Photo: 72; Fremdenverkehrsamt, Landeshauptstadt Muenchen, Christl Reiter Photo: 76; Fremdenverkehrsverbandes Muenchen-Oberbayern, A. Modl Photo: 15; German Tourist Information Office, Jaeger Photo: 88, Heider Photo: 125; Landesbildstelle, Berlin: 12, 107, 111, 112; Molzahn-Altheim Photo, Archives L V V Hessen: 26; Renner Photo, Archives L V V Hessen: 37; Senator fuer Haefen, Schiffahrt und Verkehr, Bremen: 101; Tourist Office, Cologne, Theo Felten Photo: 52, 150, Peter Fischer Photo: 152.

U. S. Library of Congress Cataloging in Publication Data

Wohlrabe, Raymond A
    The land and people of Germany.

    (Portraits of the nations series)
    SUMMARY: Introduces the geography, history, economy, culture, and people of the land known today as two countries, the Federal Republic of Germany and the German Democratic Republic.


    1. Germany—Juvenile literature. [1. Germany]
I. Krusch, Werner E., joint author. II. Title.
DD17.W6    1972        914.3/03/87        75-37248
ISBN-0-397-31261-X        ISBN-0-397-31180-X (lib. bdg.)

# Contents

# The Land and People of
# GERMANY

# 1

## The Land and the People

Germany, a land of many contrasts, has experienced marked changes in recent years. New ways of doing things have been introduced into the lives of her people. However, in the small villages and the countryside customs of earlier times have to some degree survived. The grim lessons learned from two world wars have brought democracy to the Federal Republic of Germany in the west, but the German Democratic Republic, like other Soviet-occupied territories, is still governed by a single party exerting rigid control. New problems confront both east and west. Youth has voiced an interest in politics, the economy, freedom of the individual, and departures from established customs. It is a new Germany which, despite its present state of flux and the uncertainties about its future, has forged ahead to become a leading nation in the world and the most prosperous in Europe.

Germany spreads southward from the Danish peninsula, the North Sea, and the Baltic across the heart of central Europe to the borders of Switzerland, Austria, and Czechoslovakia. West of it lie the Netherlands, Belgium, Luxembourg, and France. To the east are Poland and Czechoslovakia. The remainder of prewar Germany lies east of the Oder and Neisse rivers and is under Polish administration, except for a part of East Prussia administered directly by the Soviets. No agreement regarding reunification has been reached by the four powers, Great Britain, France, the Soviet Union, and the United States, who each occupied one of the four sectors formed at the end of World War

II. None of the nations of the Western World has accorded diplomatic recognition to the German Democratic Republic, although it has been recognized by those of the Communist bloc and other Communist countries like Yugoslavia and Cuba. The Soviet Union still maintains a military force estimated at twenty divisions within East Germany. Final boundaries must await the drafting of a treaty of peace.

In 1970 West German Chancellor Willy Brandt and Soviet Premier Alexei Kosygin signed a nonaggression pact which accepts the Oder-Neisse Line as the eastern frontier with Poland. To become valid it must be ratified by the legislative bodies of both the Federal Republic of Germany and the Soviet Union. Great opposition to the terms of the pact in West Germany, since they indirectly imply relinquishing all claim to former German territories, casts doubt upon the final outcome.

Germany has been experiencing boundary changes more or less regularly throughout her history. In recent decades the goals of her leaders had been to make her a country with boundaries enclosing all areas populated largely by Germans and excluding areas populated by other nationalities. Despite the efforts of Bismarck and Hitler, these goals have never been reached. One historian describes the periodic shrinking and expanding of the country in this way: "In a thousand years, geographic Germany has gone in and out like a concertina."

The land consists of plains, plateaus, marshlands, and mountain ranges. The highest peaks are in the Alps. Only a fringe of this mountain system extends into Germany, along the southern border. Its ranges taper into the Bavarian Plateau. Central Germany is a patchwork of forests, mountains, and river valleys that lead into the plains and marsh country farther north. Reaching to the sea and into East Germany is the North German Plain, a flat region dotted with lakes and hilly plateaus. The North Sea coastal area contrasts sharply with the shore of the Baltic. The North Sea is stormy in winter and floods across a shelf of mud flats except where dikes have been built to shut out incoming waves. About a thousand years ago this flat coastal region reached westward to the North Frisian Islands. Since then the coast has been sinking, and shallow waters lie between the mainland and these islands. Deep inlets were gouged from the mainland by the sea creating such well-protected harbors as Emden, Wilhelmshaven, and Bremerhaven. Frequent fogs are a hazard to navigation along the North Sea coast, but winter temperatures are relatively mild so that harbors are never closed by ice. The shore of the Baltic is sandy and smooth. Cliffs face the sea where there is dune country and spits form in the estuaries. The Baltic is an almost landlocked body of water linked with the North Sea by the channels of the Kattegat and Skagerrak that skirt the northern tip of Denmark. Consequently this sea has no tides, and since its waters are diluted by the many rivers that flow into it, they are about a third as salty as the waters of the North Sea.

As long ago as the Middle Ages, canals were built to supplement rivers as avenues for transportation across parts of Germany. In the fourteenth century the people of Luebeck built a canal which led from that great port to the salt deposits of the Lueneburg district. It provided a convenient way of bringing salt out on barges for shipment to other ports. The Kiel Canal provides a shortcut from the Baltic to the North Sea, eliminating the need to use the route through the Kattegat and Skagerrak. Coal barges make use of the Dortmund-Ems Canal and the Rhine-Herne Canal in the industrial region of the Ruhr Valley. The Mittelland Canal links the Dortmund-Ems Canal with the Weser and Elbe rivers to form one of the great commercial waterways of central Germany.

West Germany, an industrial nation, requires world markets for its many products. It has large coal deposits south of the Ruhr and in the Saar Basin. There are some iron deposits, ample water supplies in the Rhine and Elbe basins, and extensive potash deposits in central Germany. These are basic materials for the country's major industries such as steelmaking, the manufacture of machinery, and the production of chemicals. Since World War II the glass industries from Sudetenland, a region now a part of Czechoslovakia, have moved into eastern Bavaria. Toymaking has been centered in Nuremberg for many decades, although toys are made also in other parts of the country. In this German "toy capital" the first pocket watch, the "Nuremberg egg," was made by Peter Henlein. Clocks, jewelry, watches, and cameras are produced in great quantities. Leather goods, ceramics, fine china, and many kinds of precision and optical instruments are also major products. The town of Solingen was making the world's finest swords in the fourteenth century and today is a producer of fine cutlery.

The Federal Republic of Germany, including West Berlin, has an area of 95,937 square miles. This is almost twice the size of New York State. Its population is over sixty million. The German Democratic Republic has an area of 41,659 square miles and the population is slightly more than seventeen million. Combine these two parts of Germany and the total size is approximately half that of Texas. This does

Congress Hall in West Berlin.

not include the part of prewar Germany east of the Oder-Neisse Line.

There have been many changes in this country since World War II, particularly in West Germany. These are most evident in the big cities and large towns. Prosperity, technological advances, and an upsurge in travel are largely responsible. Family ties are strong, despite the revolt of some youths against authority and firmly established customs. However, farming methods, customs, and the use of leisure time are much the same as they have been for decades in the villages and regions where agriculture is the major interest.

More families are living in apartments today than in the past. When the debris of war-ravaged urban centers was cleared away there was an urgent need for a vast number of housing units that could be built from available materials. The apartment house met this need most economically. The German housewife has always been known to be fussy. She sweeps, scrubs, dusts, and polishes for hours to keep the home tidy and clean. Recent years of prosperity have brought more electrical appliances into the home and cut the hours needed for housework so drastically that many housewives find time for employment in industry or business. Out in the villages, doorsteps are scrubbed, the big pillowlike bedcovers bulge over the ledges of open windows on sunny days for a thorough airing, and the walks and street in front of every house are swept each Saturday. Bric-a-brac and furniture are cleaned and the living room, the showplace for guests who might drop in, is made spotless.

Cooking has always been a favorite activity of German women and the pleasure of shopping is a close second. Canned foods have become extremely popular in recent years. Most brands on the shelves of grocery stores and supermarkets are imported from the United States. Frozen foods are also in demand, with frozen spinach a favorite. Strawberries, oranges from Spain, and peaches from Italy are among the plentiful fruits. Near the top of the shopping list are green leafy lettuce, tomatoes, and cucumbers—the ingredients of the German salad. In most food stores these vegetables are available throughout the year. They are grown in the hothouses of Weismoor during the winter months. Shopping housewives make frequent visits to the sausage shops and, for a break in the routine, to their favorite *konditorei,* where only pastries, ice cream, and coffee are served.

There was an extreme shortage of automobiles available to the public even several years after the war. Slowly the manufacturers have narrowed the gap between ordering and delivery. But even today the purchaser waits several months or a year before he receives notice his car has arrived. This is why German men give their cars such meticulous care. A common sight on Saturdays along the side streets of big cities like Hamburg, Duesseldorf, and Munich is the car-washing and polishing activities of the men in a family.

An automobile makes possible a weekend picnic or a drive to a forest or lake. There the car can be parked and the whole family can hike along the network of trails that are maintained in the most picturesque parts of Germany for those who love the out-of-doors. Others drive to their *Schrebergarten* (garden plot) on the edge of the city. Some plots have a shed where the owner can stay overnight. *Schrebergarten* permit city-dwellers to enjoy a hobby that also provides them with an abundance of fresh vegetables and flowers. The automobile is also used for holiday trips to distant places. The German people have always been enthusiastic about travel. In recent years the number of German tourists who visit other countries of Europe has increased tremendously. Spain, Italy, and Yugoslavia are countries most often selected for a summer holiday. Germany has hundreds of camping places in picturesque valleys along the shores of lakes and winding streams. They accommodate swarms of campers who pitch tents or park trailers and remain for a weekend or several days.

On camping trips, after school hours, and during the summer months German youngsters play the games that are dear to their hearts. *Fuessball* (soccer) is favored by boys throughout the whole country, and handball is a favorite of teen-agers and adults. *Schlagball,* similar to baseball except that there are no bases in the game, is also popular. But the game that is watched or played by both young and old, the national game, is soccer.

The Zugspitze—highest peak in Germany.

For many generations German children have been thrilled by the books about the American West written by Karl May (1842–1912). This author was born and raised in Saxony. About fifteen of the nearly one hundred books he wrote were adventure stories with Apaches, Navajos, and Comanches rampaging through the narrative. In many of them old Chief Winnetou, a fascinating character, took a major role. *Old Sure-Hand* and *The Treasure in the Silver Lake* are two favorites. It is amazing how vividly and accurately May portrayed Indians and the life of the Old West, since he did not visit America until after all of his Indian stories had been published. German youngsters not only read May's books over and over again, but also delighted in dressing up as Indians and enacting some of the stories. In recent years the great interest in May's Indian stories convinced German movie producers that films about the American West with its Indians and cowboys would be equally fascinating. They proved to be a big success.

There are motion picture theaters in almost every city and town of West Germany. For years after the end of World War II the major screen attractions offered the German public were made by American or British producers. Today the German movie companies, which have grown rapidly in recent times, are producing an ever-increasing number of excellent films. German film producers have followed Hollywood's example in making awards each year for the best picture, the best actors, and the best actresses. The German award is called Bambi, however, instead of Oscar.

All Germans love the opera, concerts, and symphonies. This interest stems from the time when the land was ruled by kings, dukes, and counts who vied with each other in building theaters, concert halls, and opera houses so that their subjects might enjoy and appreciate fine music. Today the custom has been continued by federal, *Land* (state), and municipal governments, which set aside funds for the construction of theaters and opera houses and for subsidizing orchestras and theatrical and operatic companies. Admission to this type of entertainment costs considerably less than in the United States because of this government subsidy. Thousands from all walks of life make it a habit to enjoy an opera or a symphony concert often.

Since the end of the Nazi period West Germans have been free to attend the church of their choice and take part in religious activities. Under Hitler, Catholic priests and Protestant pastors were severely restricted. Those who were critical of the Fuehrer or his government were arrested by the Gestapo and sent to either a concentration camp or an extermination center. Records show that at least a thousand clergymen were put to death in the extermination center at Dachau alone. Monasteries and convents were seized and closed during the Nazi years, church youth organizations were banned, and religious publications suppressed. The Nazi substitute for the Christian religion was a religion based upon pagan myths and a German national church that glorified Nazi ideals. When Nazi rule ended and the church bells rang again, German people flocked to Mass or Sunday sermons in response to the call to worship.

Their experiences during World War II reduced tensions that had once existed between Catholics and Protestants. They had suffered together from the policies of the totalitarian government under Adolf Hitler. They had worked together against their common enemy. After the war thousands of refugees came to West Germany from Silesia, East Germany, the Sudetenland, and other Soviet-occupied territories. Most of the emigrés were Protestants. Thousands of them settled in regions that had been predominantly Catholic. The church is tolerated in East Germany but, since Communist governments are opposed to Christianity, the church is never encouraged and is constantly under surveillance.

West Germans must declare their religious preference in their income tax reports. The Basic Law, which is the constitution of the Federal Republic, guarantees religious freedom and prohibits the establishment of a state church. Only Catholic and Protestant churches receive federal support to supplement the contributions they receive. This comes from the *Kirchensteuer* (church tax) collected with the income tax and consequently withheld from wages and salaries. One who can prove he is an atheist does not pay this tax. Over ninety percent of the citizens of the republic pay the kirchensteuer.

Marked changes have occurred in the attitude of many of the youngsters and university students of contemporary Germany. Before World War II, Germany was a land where the parent maintained strict discipline in child rearing. The father was the symbol of authority; his opinions and demands were seldom, if ever, challenged. In towns and villages a teacher or a clergyman a youngster might meet on the street was greeted very humbly with a respectful bow. A university rector (president) was addressed as *Magnifizenz* and a dean as *Spektabilitaet,* and their decisions were final. Professors lectured in their classrooms while students obediently took notes. It was the professor's privilege to determine what subject matter should be included in a course and students' opinions or questions were seldom considered. Many of today's young people have revolted against such authority in the family, the educational institutions, the government, and the police. There have been demonstrations, sit-ins, and university building take-overs in Frankfurt, Bonn, and West Berlin. In both parts of this divided land many youths lean to the left in their thinking and, because of the subtle influence of some, a general anti-American attitude has developed. Both parts of Germany have the equivalent of American "hippies." They are called *Gammlers*. Although they do not necessarily imitate the American hippie in habits and dress, their aims and way of life correspond.

In contrast to the trend of student activists, some of the men enrolled in certain large universities have brought about the revival of the *Korporationen* or *Burschenschaften*. These organizations, which in some ways are similar to our college fraternities, were banned in the early years of the postwar period because many of their members were anti-Semitic, and they practiced *Mensur*. Mensur is the custom of dueling to settle arguments, and to obtain the distinctive scar on the cheek or forehead, which was a mark of prestige. Shortly after the war these organizations were permitted, but the practice of mensur was still banned. Eventually, it too was revived, not in all korporationen, but in a few. Relaxation of these restrictions was probably encouraged by former graduates who had come into positions of considerable influence in law, theology, medicine, and other fields—the "old boys" or, in German, the *alte Herren*.

Germany is a changed land—progressive and prosperous. Her people vow that a Hitler shall never again come to power, and they are hopefully making their new democracy secure.

# 2

# Folk Wanderings

During the Old Stone Age a race of people represented to us by Heidelberg man roamed through central Europe. They were a muscular, brutelike people with large jaws, sloping foreheads, and protruding teeth, who moved from place to place in search of food and shelter. A jawbone of one of these prehistoric nomads was uncovered by workmen in a sandpit near Heidelberg in 1907.

After thousands of years another prehistoric race appeared in the dark forests and marshlands of central Europe. These newcomers were much shorter. They walked with stooped shoulders. Their necks were short and thick and their muscles were suited to wielding clubs. Skeletons of these people were found in Neanderthal, a valley near Duesseldorf. Scientists pieced together specimens, and examined the earth where they were found. They were convinced that Neanderthal people were wanderers who used caves merely as temporary shelters, hunted for food instead of producing it, and never built homes.

In the New Stone Age the first known settlers in what is now Germany appeared. This was thousands of years after the Old Stone Age. They felled trees with crude tools fashioned from bronze, and in small clearings in the forest they built huts. Some lived in caves. These people cultivated a few plants for food.

Toward the end of this age, a slow movement of Germanic tribes began out of Europe's northern grasslands into the vast wilderness to the south and west. The migrations followed two main routes. One route led to the Rhine; the other, to the Danube River and the Black Sea. Some tribes settled near the Elbe River and along the shores of the Baltic Sea. They built huts on pilings in the lakes of the region to protect themselves from attack by hostile neighbors or hungry animals. Traders who ventured north beyond the Mediterranean brought back strange tales. Pliny, a Roman writer of the first century, described the people on the shores of the Baltic as having hooves like horses and ears like elephants!

Germanic warriors east of the Rhine were fierce fighters who wore the skins of animals fastened over their shoulders. They were tall, with blue eyes and flowing blond hair. In battle they usually wore the heads of wolves or cattle on their helmets. Constant warfare prevented them from building villages, so their huts were clustered in forest clearings and their cattle pastured close by. Family fought family; tribe waged war on tribe.

When the Roman Empire expanded toward this wilderness, barbarians learned about Roman ways and customs. Eventually they were permitted to settle in Roman territory and serve in the Roman army. Some became officers or held positions of trust in the civil government. Romans, during this period, were not happy about serving as soldiers. They preferred to enjoy the luxuries of life at home. The empire was growing soft and weak and was spread over vast areas. Slaves and wealth were pouring in from the provinces, and the free farming class was rapidly dwindling. Conflict with the barbarians was inevitable.

The first major test of Roman strength came in 102 B.C. when chieftains of the Germanic Cimbrian tribes were temporarily successful in an attack along the northern frontier of the empire. But they were eventually defeated by the military skill of the Roman leader Marius.

Almost a hundred years later Hermann, a young chieftain of the Germanic Cheruscan tribe, won a major victory over the Romans. Hermann was known to the Romans as Arminius. He had been entrusted with a command in the army assigned to the lower Rhine valley. While on an expedition in the wilderness, in A.D. 9, he plotted with dissatisfied tribal leaders to kill Varus, the Roman governor. The legions of Varus were trapped in the Teutoburg Forest and both hostile barbarians and disloyal Roman soldiers joined in the massacre. When Varus saw how disastrous was his defeat he fell on his sword and died. The emperor Augustus, frightened by the loss of the army, withdrew the frontier of the empire to the Rhine River.

Augustus's decision was responsible for the construction of the *Limes* from Koblenz on the Rhine to the city of Regensburg on the Danube. The Limes was a wall, second in size only to the Great Wall of China,

Entrance to the Roman military camp, Saalburg, a reconstruction near Bad Homburg in Hesse.

built to protect Roman territory from the hordes of barbarians in the north and east. In many places it was fifty feet thick at the base. Towers were built at frequent intervals to permit the use of signal fires. The wall was nearly 350 miles long. As further precautions, river boats patrolled the Rhine below Koblenz, and Roman legions were stationed at Bonn, Strassburg, Mainz, and other strategic points.

It was not long before the barbarians facing the frontiers of the empire grew restless again. The victory won by Hermann had taught them that Romans could be outwitted, outfought, and forced to yield. Along the lower Rhine were the Franks, a Germanic tribe formed by the union of the small tribes of the northern wilderness. The forests across the Rhine to the south became the homeland of the Alemanni, another union of small tribes. These barbarians learned about the cities, the mild climate, and the luxuries the Romans enjoyed, from tribesmen who had lived within the boundaries of the empire. They longed to move into the more desirable Mediterranean region.

In A.D. 167 the Marcomanni from Bohemia and the Quadi from Moravia, both Germanic tribes, invaded Roman territory. They broke across the frontier along the Danube and entered what is now northern Italy. Sixty years later the Alemanni broke through the Limes between the Rhine and the Danube. They were followed by the Franks who crossed the lower Rhine into Gaul (now France).

The Goths began a slow migration, in the third century, from the valley of the Oder into the Balkans. Crude wagons were used to carry household goods; women and children walked. Fierce Goth horsemen guarded the caravans. They eventually entered Greece. The vast horde split into two groups—the Visigoths and the Ostrogoths. Both were soon converted to Christianity by Ulfilas, a Roman missionary of Gothic origin who had invented an alphabet so that portions of the Bible could be translated into Gothic. The Alemanni swarmed into the Rhineland, and the Burgundians and Vandals moved into the valley of the Main.

The fourth century saw the beginning of the greatest invasion of Europe by barbarians. Far to the east the Huns began moving westward.

To escape from the path of these merciless horsemen from the steppes of Mongolia, the Slavs pressed hard upon the Germanic tribes. Near the start of the fifth century the appearance of the Huns caused an invasion of the Roman Empire by the Visigoths. Under King Alaric, the Visigoths sacked Rome in A.D. 410, and then wandered into Spain, which had been invaded by the Vandals a few years before. After Alaric's death the Visigoths settled in Spain and central Gaul, and the Vandals moved into Africa. The floodgates had been opened wide! The sea of Germanic tribes—Franks, Alemanni, Goths, and Vandals —swarmed over the once powerful empire of the Romans.

Near the middle of the fifth century, Attila, king of the Huns, appeared in western Europe. He invaded the Rhineland and Gaul and conquered some Germanic tribes, but his success was short-lived. Romans and Germans, fighting side by side, drove him and his wild horsemen back across the Rhine. In 452 Attila began his march toward Rome. It is said that Pope Leo I journeyed from Rome to Attila's camp and warned him to advance no farther. He reminded Attila that others who had invaded and sacked the city had died shortly after. The pope's warning was heeded and the dreaded army of barbarians withdrew. A year later Attila died and his empire fell apart.

At the dawn of the fifth century, the western lands of the Roman Empire were held by tribes from the grasslands of northern Europe. In just a few hundred years these barbaric people had adopted Roman ways and had accepted Christianity. Despite the breaking up of the empire, they endeavored to preserve much of the culture they had greatly admired—the laws, the language, and the way of life of the Romans.

# 3

# Life in the Middle Ages

During the Middle Ages the life of the people who inhabited Germany was shaped by the power struggle among feudal lords. Small-scale conflicts and major wars were both rife. Security of home, property, and life had reached a low level. Men of wealth and influence built castles designed as bulwarks against foes who sought to expand their domains or replenish their coffers by surprise attacks. The common people built their homes, mere hovels in those days, huddled close below the castle of the man they served in return for the privilege of living on his land.

Turmoil was due largely to the greed of the men who were leaders. Amid the crosscurrents of the flood of barbaric tribes deluging the frontier lands of the Roman Empire, a few definite islands of strength began to form. The Alemanni controlled the upper Rhinelands. The Bavarians had settled on the plains just north of the Alps. The might of the Saxons was centered between the Rhine, the Weser, and the Elbe rivers. Frisians held the islands and marshlands of the northwest coast between what now is the Netherlands and Denmark. The Franks held the lower Rhineland, and the Thuringians the central part of East Germany. Then, through wars of conquest, the Franks expanded the boundaries of their domain to include the lands of all of these peoples. The emperor of the Franks, Charlemagne, waged a bitter war against the Saxons. He destroyed their pagan gods and temples, converted them to Christianity, and brought them into the Frankish Empire. The union was short-lived. Upon the death of Charlemagne's grandsons, the empire fell apart. In the following centuries power was in the hands of men whose lands and family ties enabled them to create strong tribal duchies.

Settlement of the great wilderness began in earnest about A.D. 800. This was the beginning of the era many historians call the Age of Forest Clearance. For a period of over four hundred years large tracts of forest were cleared, and vast areas of marsh and heathlands were converted to useful soil. Towns also began to rise in the wilderness.

Medieval towns originated in three different ways. Some grew from settlements that had been used by the Romans as outposts beyond the frontiers of their empire. Others began as clusters of peasants' huts huddled close to some nobleman's castle, a church, or a monastery. Some sprang from the union of three or four settlements where vital trade routes crossed.

During the Middle Ages in Germany, as in all of Europe, the feudal system prevailed in political, economic, and social life. A nobleman, his headquarters usually a castle, provided protection for the peasants who were his tenants. The peasants made payments for the privilege of using his land by contributing a large share of what they produced to him. In order to pay for the lord's protection they worked and lived like slaves.

The castles crowning Rhineland hilltops today, some crumbling and covered with vines, were built in the latter part of the Middle Ages. Castles now in ruins in many other parts of the land were built about the same time. Their construction was possible only after stonecutters had learned the skills from artisans of Mediterranean countries. Castles built earlier in the western wilderness resembled the wooden forts of pioneer days in America.

These first castles were not elaborate. A hilltop was the usual site, chosen because it afforded a view of any approaching danger. A moat was dug and a wall of closely fitting logs was placed along its inner edge. Then the towers and the house of the nobleman were constructed. They contained none of the luxuries we usually associate

A medieval castle in ruins, Castle Muenzenberg in Hesse.

with castles built in the latter part of the medieval period. Since there was no glass, windows were mere slits covered with glazed linen. Tables were made of planks. The nobleman and his guests sat on stools, not chairs. Straw was spread on the floor in winter. The food was simple, without spices, and cooked on a spit in the fireplace. Beds were hung with heavy curtains of wool to shut out the night air, and mattresses were filled with straw. Until the twelfth century lavish furnishings were unknown.

Once the Crusaders returned from the wars in the Holy Land, during the latter part of the eleventh century to the end of the thirteenth, castles became more substantial, more elaborate. The main gateway, set in a huge tower, was reached by a drawbridge that spanned a deep moat. The entrance was protected by a portcullis, a heavy iron grating suspended by chains, that could be lowered to serve as a barricade in case of attack. Between the towers were high walls of stone, ten to twenty feet thick. Bastioned towers provided vantage points overlooking the courtyard inside the walls, and the surrounding countryside. The central and strongest part of the castle was both a fortress and the residence of the nobleman. Rugs replaced the straw formerly used on the floor and rich tapestries were hung on the walls. In the banquet hall the food was tastier because of the introduction of spices and condiments. Forks eliminated the need to eat with the fingers and there was a marked improvement in manners.

The homes of the serfs who lived outside the walls of a castle were thatched houses with earthen floors and no windows. Only in the castle was there candlelight at night. Food was cooked over an open fire in the center of the room, and the smoke escaped through a hole in the thatched roof. The peasants' days were filled by work in the fields. There were few pleasures or amusements. Only the nobleman and his retainers had time for hunting, waging war, or building castles.

There was little security or protection from danger in medieval times. Anyone who ventured out at night was liable to be robbed. Few people traveled because there were few, if any, roads; the Roman highways built of stone had been destroyed through centuries of use without repair. Travelers did well to join a guarded caravan of merchants for protection. Many of the bands of robbers roving over the countryside consisted of knights. On some of the trade routes a toll, usually paid in goods, was exacted for permission to cross a nobleman's lands. Rivers used as avenues of commerce by merchants were subject to toll by unscrupulous barons, who often plundered the wares of those not well protected.

Certain rights were granted to large towns formed by the fusion of small villages, to benefit their merchants and burghers. Some became imperial cities which owed allegiance only to the emperor. The largest cities had streets that were narrow lanes, were walled, and were surrounded by a moat for greater protection. Within the area enclosed by a city's walls were a town hall, marketplaces, shops, and houses. In most of the large towns the craftsmen and merchants were organized in guilds.

No strong central power existed in the land of the Germanic peoples

Houses were often built on bridges during the Middle Ages. A few of them still stand in parts of Germany.

A medieval town hall in the little town of Alsfeld, Hesse.

during the Middle Ages. There were kings, and some of the kings became emperors of the Holy Roman Empire. But the real power was in the hands of the dukes who controlled the tribal duchies. A king had to gain the support of these men if he wished to have any real authority in his kingdom. Only a few outstanding leaders arose, among them King Otto I, and Frederick Barbarossa, who lost his life while leading his army of Crusaders in the Holy Land.

There were few changes during the centuries of the Middle Ages in this part of Europe. The Gutenberg Bible was printed in Mainz. Alchemists were busy with their struggle to find the philosopher's stone which they believed would turn the baser metals to gold. Better armor was made for knights; better swords and crossbows were designed. Late in the period an upsurge in trade brought prosperity to the burghers of some cities. Trade fairs and festivals brightened the life of the people. The Black Death stalked across Europe, killing perhaps half of the total population. Paganism was stamped out but superstition, born of ignorance, took its place. Slowly through the centuries the common people began to win privileges that lifted them above the status of mere serfs.

# 4

## Religious Wars

Visitors swarmed in the marketplace of the little town of Wittenberg on the eve of All Saints' Day in 1517. A man clad in the robes of an Augustinian monk walked through the crowd. He went straight to the Castle Church, a Gothic structure towering above thatched huts and the walls of the town. On the church door he nailed a list of ninety-five propositions he wished his fellow faculty members of the University of Wittenberg to consider for discussion. Posting such notices on the church door had been a custom of long standing. His ninety-five statements dealt with abuses of church practices. Historians have listed that monk, Martin Luther, as one of Germany's greatest men.

Luther's condemnation of abuses in the sale of indulgences set in motion the forces leading to the Reformation and Counter-Reformation, a long period of bitter religious turmoil. An indulgence is a pardon from temporal punishment for sin. Such a pardon comes through good works, prayer, fasting, giving of alms, and repentance. Men who joined the armies of Christendom in the wars against the infidel during the Crusades were rewarded in this way. Those who were unable to join could make donations to gain indulgences. When the period of the Crusades had passed, indulgences were granted in return for contributions of gold, jewels, and other valuables. Archbishops were permitted to delegate the task of collecting the contributions.

It was a Dominican monk, John Tetzel, who took charge of this work for the archbishop of Mainz. Tetzel sold pardons for many sins the church had never intended to include, a practice which irked men like Luther. Many disliked the way he used threats and ballyhoo to increase his sales. Martin Luther raised his voice against such flagrant abuse of church practices.

News of the ninety-five theses spread throughout Germany. Luther was surprised at the response. The archbishop of Mainz was furious. He reprimanded Tetzel and ordered Luther to appear before Pope Leo X in Rome.

Martin Luther was a subject of Frederick the Wise, Elector of Saxony. Frederick refused to permit the arrest of the monk, because he deemed it unsafe for him to leave German territory. A meeting in Augsburg was arranged, with Cardinal de Vio representing the pope. At this meeting, Luther humbled himself before the high-ranking church official but stuck firmly to his convictions. The cardinal demanded that he recant; the monk refused. It was not safe for him to remain in Augsburg, so he fled under cover of darkness.

The death of Emperor Maximilian I of the Holy Roman Empire shifted the spotlight of attention away from the Wittenberg monk for a while. But debates continued over the question of church practices. Luther wrote volumes explaining his views, and printing presses provided excerpts in leaflet form for a vast audience of knights, nobles, and burghers. The princes were concerned at the time over the imperial election. Each contender spent great sums to create a show of wealth, power, and pomp. The electors decided on young Charles V, Habsburg king of Spain. Charles was chosen only after the prince obtained his promise to respect the rights of Germans. The election over, attention drifted again to the monk and his writings.

A papal bull, which is a decree from the pope, was issued, branding Luther a heretic. It demanded his books be burned, and placed the ban of the empire on any prince who gave him aid. Papal legates who brought the document northward met with varied receptions. Feeling ran high in the little university town. Wittenberg students publicly burned a copy of the bull.

In 1521, the attention of all Europe was focused on ancient Worms.

Princes with splendid retinues swarmed to the meeting of the German diet (assembly) called by Emperor Charles. Knights, royal attendants in colorful liveries, and papal dignitaries crowded the streets. Luther was to appear before the diet to defend his stand. By this time condemnation had gone far beyond the matter of indulgences. Along the route to Worms crowds met Luther at the gates of cities, and hundreds climbed to walls, trees, and housetops for a better view of him.

Meetings of the diet were held in the palace near the cathedral in Worms. So crowded were the streets, Luther had to be guided through gardens and side lanes to reach the assembly hall. He trembled during his first appearance before the emperor and the princes and ecclesiastical leaders assembled to hear him. He asked for more time to consider. But at his second appearance he spoke out boldly and refused to recant. Emperor Charles signed an edict which placed on him the ban of the empire.

Frederick the Wise knew that Luther's life was now in grave danger and also knew he must avoid the consequences of openly helping the reformer. A plot was devised whereby Luther was to be kidnapped on his journey back to Wittenberg. As his carriage threaded its way through the Thuringian Forest, knights in ambush halted it, seized the monk and took him secretly to Wartburg Castle. In this safe hideout Luther's time was not wasted. He began one of the major contributions of his life—the translation of the Bible into German. In March, 1522, he heard of the wild disorders being blamed on his teachings and decided it was time to return to Wittenberg.

Luther had preached against wrongs both he and large numbers of Catholics felt should be corrected. The misinterpretation of his sermons and writing fanned into flame the smoldering grievances of all classes. It kindled revolt of such proportions that most of Europe was drawn into the turmoil to be scarred by war, destruction, hatred, and mob violence. Three major strata of German society were in arms against one another or against the Roman Catholic church.

There were wars between the knights of the empire and the princes. One of the leaders, Franz von Sickingen, an adventurous robber-

One of the famous thatched-roof houses of the Black Forest.

knight, led an army of knights in a daring attack against the archbishop of Trier. Philip of Hesse and the Elector of the Palatinate came to the archbishop's aid with their well-equipped armies. The knights, with outmoded armor and weapons, were no match for this superior force. They were routed and withdrew to Landstuhl Castle, one of von Sickingen's many castles, where they and their leader met defeat and disaster.

The German peasants broadened Luther's demands for religious freedom to include freedom from all the ills that had been their lot. They banded together under the emblem of the *Bundschuh* (the peasant's shoe), a sign that soon struck fear into the hearts of nobles and wealthy burghers.

The Peasants' War began in 1524 near the Black Forest. It spread rapidly throughout much of southern and central Germany. An arbitrary act of the wife of a nobleman started the revolt: she insisted her peasants gather snail shells in the forest at the peak of the harvest when they were hard pressed for time to bring in their crops. Hans Mueller, leader of the peasants, rode through the villages of southern Germany demanding that all join in the uprising. Bands of peasants with all manner of weapons waged war on the nobility and the church. In Franconia and Wuerttemberg hundreds of castles were burned to the ground and scores of monasteries were destroyed. Works of art were demolished or damaged. Murder and torture were rife. Finally, the armies of the league of Swabian cities and of powerful princes united to put down the revolt. Thousands of peasants were annihilated, hundreds tortured and beheaded. The war ended a year after it started and the peasants lost the few rights and freedoms they had possessed.

Accusations that his teaching was responsible for the peasant revolt infuriated Martin Luther. He had advocated prayer, not force and bloodshed, for gaining new freedoms and correcting abuses. But he appealed to the nobles to use any means, force and bloodshed included, to quell the rebels. To the peasant class, who firmly believed he would champion their cause, this was a surprising about-face. It was a disappointment they could not forgive. It resulted in a decline in popularity for Protestantism.

The princes formed the third warring group in the conflict. In southern Germany, the princes were almost entirely on the side of the Roman Catholic church and the emperor. In other parts of the land, they formed the opposition. Clashes between the two factions filled the decades between the Peasants' War and the end of the Thirty Years' War in 1648. There was a short lull when Suleiman the Magnificent threatened invasion of central Europe by Turkish warriors. This brought a peace treaty, signed in Nuremberg in 1532, so that Catholics and Protestants might join against this common enemy from the East. The brilliant action of the defenders of the tiny fortress of Guens in a mountain pass along Suleiman's route held his army at bay, and the approach of winter prevented him from continuing his march to Vienna.

Diets met several times during these decades. Each made a futile attempt to settle differences. A major stumbling block was the confiscation of Catholic church property by territorial princes with large Protestant majorities in their realms. Many churches and monasteries were transferred from ecclesiastical to secular or civil control. The diets were held in large cities designated by the emperor. To these meeting places flocked the princes, bishops, and electors, and the magistrates of imperial cities. But a prince, if he wished, could ignore a summons to attend. The danger of his being punished if he opposed the laws of the diet was not great. Usually such action was punished by placing him under the ban of the empire. This meant little if other members of the diet refused to help in enforcing it.

The disastrous Thirty Years' War had several causes. Germany, not yet a nation, was a conglomeration of principalities under rulers bound loosely to the edicts of the Holy Roman Empire. The emperor had little power. Enmity between Catholics and Protestants had been intensified by persecutions on both sides. The war broke out over an incident in Bohemia where Rudolph II had granted certain religious freedoms by royal charter.

The historical record of this conflict is one of battles, brutality, starvation, and intrigue. It left a swath of destruction across the heart of the continent. In the first major engagement, the Battle of the White Mountain in Bohemia in 1620, Duke Maximilian of Bavaria and Count von Tilly, his general, won a victory. Then a wealthy Bohemian nobleman, Albrecht von Wallenstein, joined on the side of the Roman Catholic church and the emperor. Wallenstein required the peasants and burghers to supply provisions and contributions for his army. Where his soldiers went, farms and villages were plundered.

Down from the north came Gustavus Adolphus, king of Sweden. He was an ardent Lutheran who had won victories over Poland and Pomerania on the shores of the Baltic. At about the same time, the city of Magdeburg, an ancient cultural center, was destroyed by fire during an attack by Catholic forces. Enraged Protestants joined the army of the Swedish king by the thousands.

Castle ruins in Eppstein, a Hessian village in the Taunus Mountains.

The plight of both sides grew worse as the war continued. In the Battle of Breitenfeld, Tilly suffered a defeat. Emperor Ferdinand dismissed Wallenstein from the command of his army. In a battle in the Lech valley Tilly lost his life. Gustavus Adolphus moved on to take Nuremberg and Munich.

Again Wallenstein entered the conflict. The emperor induced him to return and lead the imperial army against the forces of the Swedish king. In the Battle of Luetzen in Saxony, in 1632, Wallenstein was defeated, but Gustavus Adolphus lost his life. New intrigues, fanned by the Spanish ambassador to the imperial court in Vienna, brought a charge of treason against Wallenstein. Finally, a plot to assassinate the general was successful.

A new phase of the war began when the emperor's son, the young king of Hungary, assumed command of the Catholic army. Cities of southern Germany that had fallen into Protestant hands were retaken. France had supplied troops and funds for the aid of German princes in the Protestant camp. She now boldly maneuvered to accomplish her real purpose—the conquest of the territory along the Rhine. Spanish troops bolstered the forces of the emperor. The enmity between German princes dimmed somewhat when they saw their land becoming a battleground for foreign troops, and Frenchmen and Swedes uniting to plunder German cities. A diet met in Ratisbon but decided upon another meeting at a later date to draw up peace terms. Battles and shifting alliances continued while nearly four years of bickering passed. Eventually the Catholics, assembled in Muenster, and the Protestants, in Osnabrueck, agreed to the terms of the Peace of Westphalia on October 24, 1648. Boundary disputes were settled. Most important, each prince was given the right to decide the faith of his subjects.

Then a Germany devastated by thirty years of war looked upon the price it had paid. At least a third of the population was dead. Industries were ruined; commerce was at a standstill; cities laid waste were deserts of desolation. Art and literature had slumped to their lowest ebb. Germany faced the task of healing its wounds, rebuilding its castles, churches, and cities, and moving forward again.

# 5

## The Rise of Prussia

During their migration into western Europe, Teutonic peoples found no promise for the future in the region along the southern shores of the Baltic Sea. Sandy soil, dismal marshlands, sparse vegetation, and cold winds out of the north in winter were not attractive. Tales of lush valleys and dense forests prodded tribal chieftains to lead their people farther south. The Baltic lands were merely routes to their destination. Centuries later these regions became the domains of powerful kings and the core of an expanding state called Prussia.

Linked with the growth of Prussia is Castle Hohenzollern high on a mountaintop of the Swabian Alb in southern Germany. The original castle was built in the eighth century by one of the counts of Zollern. The early history of the house of Hohenzollern and Prussia is steeped in adventure, intrigue, wars, and privation. Prussia and its royal family, however, were one of the foundations of modern Germany.

The Order of Teutonic Knights, founded at Acre in Palestine during the Crusades, also contributed to the rise of Prussia. Its members, all Germans of noble birth, wore with their armor a distinctive white mantle marked with a black cross. Each had vowed to live a simple life dedicated to bringing Christianity to heathens. When the wars to win Jerusalem from the infidel subsided, their attention was turned toward the wild tribes near the Baltic Sea.

The Teutonic Knights had founded a state of their own on the Vistula River by 1237. The cities of Memel and Koenigsberg were built, and where the silt of the Vistula formed a delta the knights constructed the great fortress of Marienburg. On the heights of this stronghold a gigantic statue of the Virgin Mary was placed. Luxurious living and great wealth from their trade in wax and amber soon weakened the knights' adherence to their vows. Wars were fought against the Lithuanians, their neighbors to the north, who were still faithful to their pagan gods. Ambitious expansion of their domains brought on conflicts with the armies of the king of Poland and resulted in a major defeat at Tannenberg in 1410. Many of their castles were lost and their cities occupied.

The ambitious Hohenzollerns added new territories to their domains through marriages, wars, purchase, and treaty arrangements. Count Frederick II was made burgraviate of Nuremberg in 1192. In 1411 a Hohenzollern was appointed governor of the Mark of Brandenburg, which was still inhabited by heathen Slavs. Brandenburg's rulers became electors of the Holy Roman Empire and their votes helped decide who would wear the imperial crown.

Frontier lands were not the choicest gifts an emperor could bestow. They brought duties such as converting the inhabitants who were pagan and bringing rebellious local leaders into line. Frederick I, margrave of Brandenburg in the fifteenth century, found villages pillaged by roving bands under local leaders. When pursued, the bands fled to Freisack Castle, an impregnable fortress. Frederick borrowed a cannon from a friend, battered down the fortress walls, and put an end to their activities. His successor, Margrave Frederick II, purchased the domains of the Teutonic Knights when their fortunes were at their lowest ebb. Through both diplomacy and intrigue, Elector John Sigismund added the Duchy of Cleves and other Rhineland principalities to the Hohenzollern domains.

The Great Elector, Frederick William I (1640–1688), was faced with serious difficulties arising from the Thirty Years' War. There had been territorial losses and widespread anarchy. He reduced expenditures since he was burdened with the indemnity due to Sweden by the Treaty of Westphalia. Frederick William ruled wisely and strengthened his control over his subjects. He did much to encourage industry, promote agriculture, bring colonists from other countries and build a strong army. A canal to aid commerce was constructed to link the Spree and Oder rivers with the North Sea. Administration of Hohenzollern lands was made more effective by the acquisition of new territories to fill the gaps between existing domains.

Frederick III, who succeeded the Great Elector, squandered all of the accumulated wealth for a reign of splendor. Each event at his court in Berlin was one of pomp and ceremony. Shrewd diplomacy upon Frederick's part wrung from Emperor Leopold the imperial signature to a treaty which brought the designation of Kingdom of Prussia, a very coveted change. Elector Frederick III became King Frederick I of Prussia.

So great a change called for a dazzling display, a coronation requiring months of planning. The ceremonies began in December, 1700. A procession with thousands of fine horses and all of the princes, nobles, and their attendants left Berlin, the Hohenzollern capital, for ancient Koenigsberg. It took almost two weeks to reach this stronghold of East Prussia. More weeks were required for the ceremonies that marked the founding of the kingdom of Prussia, the installation of the members of the new Order of the Black Eagle, and the coronation. The crowning of Frederick and his queen surpassed in splendor the coronation of many an emperor.

King Frederick I was followed to the throne by his son, Frederick William I, in 1713. He was entirely different in nature—brusque, often brutal, and caring not a bit for ceremony. He put an end to extravagant spending and dismissed his father's army of courtiers. His goals were an efficient administration, absolute power for the king, and a strong nation. He was guilty of lavish spending in only one area —his regiment of giant grenadiers. His agents scoured Europe in search of men of great size. They were given fine quarters in Potsdam near Berlin and drilled on the parade grounds by the king himself.

Many stories are told of King Frederick William's abuse of his children. Often he humiliated in public the prince who was destined to succeed him to the throne. Beatings, threats, and his father's incessant raging led young Frederick to plan to escape to a foreign land. The king was suspicious and kept his son under constant guard. But while on a tour with his father in southern Germany, young Frederick decided to attempt escape. He planned to meet a friend, Hans Katte, in Holland after crossing the border into France. In the early morning hours a page entrusted to bring horses for the prince was late and the plot was discovered. The king sent for his son and ordered him imprisoned in Cuestrin Castle. Katte, despite urgent warnings to flee, awaited the officers sent to arrest him in Berlin.

This incident led to one of the most painful ordeals of Prince Frederick's life. Minute instructions were sent by the king regarding the daily routine to be followed by the prisoner during his confinement. Hans Katte was condemned to die and sent to Cuestrin Castle to await execution. When Katte was taken into the courtyard to be beheaded, the prince was forced to watch the proceedings from his cell window. This ordeal brought about a change in the young man's character. It taught him despite his dislike for his father, to show great humility and respect in his presence. When the prince became king, the trait of never revealing through his actions his intentions or feelings carried over into the field of diplomacy. Eventually, through the intercession of Emperor Leopold, the prince was released from prison.

One of young Frederick's first projects after he ascended the throne was the conquest of Silesia. Emperor Charles VI had died and Maria Theresa, his daughter, was trying desperately to hold together his vast empire. She protested Frederick's forays into Silesia. But in spite of her pleading, he entered Breslau, capital of Silesia, before she had time to dispatch an army. When the Austrians came to defend the province they were defeated. In the Treaty of Dresden in 1745, Maria Theresa ceded the province to the king of Prussia and it became another addition to the Hohenzollern domains.

A Silesian war of greater proportions, the Seven Years' War, broke out in 1756. It was another attempt by Austria to regain her former province and halt the growing power of Prussia. When peace came in

1763, neither Austria nor Prussia gained, but each had lost thousands of soldiers in battle. Prussia was saved from defeat by the brilliance, strategy, and perseverance of her king. As attempts by the older members of the European family of nations to eliminate Prussia failed, respect for the Prussian leaders increased.

King Frederick's domain now became a leading power. East Prussia and the regions along the southern shores of the Baltic changed miraculously under the Hohenzollerns. Marshlands were drained, and forests planted; roads were built, and the number of farm plots increased. In 1772 West Prussia was taken from Poland and colonists from Holland and Bohemia improved the land and built small villages. Silesia and parts of Frisia became Prussian territory. Nearly a million people, including Huguenots fleeing from persecution in France, crossed Prussian borders to settle and build homes. And so lands deemed unfit for settlement by Teutonic tribal chieftains many centuries before, became one of the great kingdoms of Europe by the eighteenth century.

# 6

## Unification and the German Empire

Boundaries of the German land, or Deutschland, have shifted drastically over the centuries. Germany is not a mere political unit. Germans prefer to think of it as a geographical area covering three distinct regions—the North German Plains, the central plateau and highlands, and the Alps. Central Europe was settled by Teutonic tribal groups between the third and fifth centuries. These settlements were later replaced by feudal principalities. Then the principalities were united by exceedingly weak bonds to form a larger political unit —an empire. Charlemagne, Frederick the Great, and Napoleon all attempted to unite the unwieldy conglomeration of three or four hundred independent dukedoms, bishoprics, and minor principalities.

Many historians point to A.D. 800 as the year that marks the beginning of the German nation. On Christmas Day of that year Charlemagne, emperor of the Franks, was crowned emperor of the Holy Roman Empire in St. Peter's in Rome by Pope Leo III. It was an act of appreciation on the part of the pope, because at one point when the pope had been driven from Rome, Charlemagne received him with a show of dazzling magnificence, espoused the pope's cause, and returned with him to Rome in order to assure his reinstatement. After his coronation, Charlemagne became another in the long line of Roman caesars with an empire embracing not only the lands of the German-speaking peoples, but also a large share of Italy, Spain, the Netherlands, Belgium, and France.

For a number of centuries Germany was part of the Holy Roman Empire whose emperors, elected by a board of princes, were not always of the same royal house. The Carolingian line, which included Charlemagne, came to an end with Arnulf of Carinthia. In 962 young Pope John XII placed the imperial crown on the head of Otto the Great, a Saxon. Frederick Barbarossa, a member of the House of Hohenstaufen, received the same honor in Rome in 1155. A number of Hohenstaufens followed him to the imperial throne. During their rule medieval Germany reached its peak of cultural development. After the death of Conrad IV, the last of this line, there was no emperor for a period of almost twenty years.

Rudolph of Habsburg was chosen by the electors in 1273. The Habsburgs ruled the Holy Roman Empire for several centuries. This

Cochem Castle and the town of Cochem on the Mosel River.

weak union of German states and Habsburg domains came to an end in 1806 when the armies of Napoleon entered Vienna. The French leader forced Emperor Francis II to renounce the imperial office and become merely emperor of Austria. The Holy Roman Empire, which was never revived, had been only a shaky union of German principalities with Austria playing the role of leader. The emperor had been emperor in name only. The real power had been in the hands of those German princes, particularly the dukes, whose families possessed extensive domains. These included the Wittelsbachs, Luxembourgs, Wettins, and Hohenzollerns. When Martin Luther broke with the Catholic church, Protestantism swept across much of Europe and German principalities drifted farther apart. The rise of the kingdom of Prussia was the next step in creating a union.

Napoleon made an attempt to unite the Germans and settle the differences between them which had a tendency to provoke war. Bishoprics and free imperial cities were abolished and their territories added to a few large German principalities in 1803. These, with the exception of Austria and Prussia, were united to form the Confederation of the Rhine. The constitution Napoleon provided abolished the nobility and their special privileges. The French emperor became presiding officer of the confederation.

Following the War of Liberation and the final defeat of Napoleon, the heads of the major European states and hundreds of diplomats attended the Congress of Vienna for the purpose of remapping Europe. One of the biggest problems they faced was the German question. What was to be done with these states to make them a stronger force in European politics? Their solution, though not entirely satisfactory, served its purpose for a while. It was the creation of a German confederation which included Prussia, Saxony, Bavaria, and all of the other German kingdoms with Austria at its head. Control was centered in a diet that met at regular intervals in Frankfurt. But with no army to enforce its decisions, the Frankfurt Diet had no authority. Constant controversy between Austria and Prussia made it still more ineffective.

The purpose in creating the confederation was to place a strong united force in the path of any future Napoleons.

The German people became restless and dissatisfied. They wanted a constitution and a representative assembly for their government. Constitutions had been promised. Except in Bavaria, Baden, and Weimar, the promises had not been kept. Metternich, the German-born chancellor of Austria, did all in his power to prevent German princes from granting the people representation.

On March 18, 1848, the atmosphere was tense in Berlin, the capital of Prussia. News of revolt in Vienna heightened the tension. Soldiers were ordered to patrol the streets of the city, but crowds swarmed in the palace courtyard and refused to disperse. King Frederick William IV ordered the soldiers to go into action. Shots were fired and a riot ensued that ended in bloodshed.

By March 19 the atmosphere in Berlin had changed. The frightened king stood with head bowed while the corpses of the slain were carried past him. In a proclamation King Frederick William promised that Prussia would join with other states to form a united Germany.

An assembly met in Frankfurt in 1849, adopted a constitution for a German empire, and offered Frederick William the crown. But he spurned the offer because it came from the common people and not from the heads of states who alone had the sovereign right to make such an offer.

After the death of King Frederick William in 1861 and the succession of William I, Otto von Bismarck, who was to become one of the greatest figures in German history, began to make himself known in German politics. He was the son of a Prussian Junker.

The Junkers, owners of large estates east of the Elbe River, were the conservative group in Prussian politics. Since their land, most of it taken from the Slavs, was probably the least productive in the realm, they worked hard managing their estates. In this group the Prussian kings found faithful servants for important positions in the army and government.

Otto von Bismarck was born April 1, 1815, in Schoenhausen, a town in Saxony. While he was still a baby his family moved to an estate of nearly two thousand acres in Pomerania, a province of Prussia on the Baltic Sea. Early in life he began to show the traits so pronounced in later years—shrewdness, conservatism, firmness, and loyalty to his king. King William made him his prime minister in 1862.

The contest between Prussia and Austria for supremacy among the German states now began in earnest. Bismarck started his long-range program to form a united Germany. His first surprising act was to ally Prussia with Austria in a war against Denmark over the Danish provinces of Schleswig and Holstein where the population was largely German. Prussian military action won a quick victory over the Danish army. The conference in London which followed brought an unsatisfactory settlement. But Bismarck was patient. Soon an excuse for an invasion of Holstein arose and Prussian troops were sent into the territory. Austria, not wishing to see Prussia expand its territory and gain prestige, strongly objected and took the Schleswig-Holstein problem to the Frankfurt Diet. Ensuing events led to war between Prussia and Austria.

Bismarck was not unprepared for such an action by his former ally. His armies first conquered some of the smaller German states and then maneuvered for an attack against the armies of the Austrian emperor. The decisive battle of the conflict was fought at Koeniggraetz. Napoleon III was asked to be the arbiter in settling the terms of peace. Prussia, the victor, was permitted to annex Holstein and most of Schleswig and to form a North German Confederation which excluded Austria.

Ironically, Bismarck's next move was against France and Napoleon III. He managed to bring about a declaration of war against Prussia by the French Assembly over an apparent slight to a French diplomat. The German states were aroused to action and sided with Prussia in the conflict. The Franco-Prussian War, with its terrible loss of life, was decided in the Battle of Sedan, fought in September, 1870. Both King William and Bismarck watched its progress from a nearby hill. Brilliant action by the German forces took the great French fortress. The prize was greater than had been expected. Included among the prisoners who surrendered was Emperor Napoleon III. He was banished and sent to Wilhelmshoehe Castle in Kassel. Before peace was signed the German army entered Paris. The French Assembly deposed their emperor and set up a republic. By the terms of the peace treaty signed in Frankfurt in 1872, Prussia was given Alsace and Lorraine and a huge indemnity to be paid by France.

Bismarck's grand plan for a united Germany was almost complete. South German states were taken into the North German Confederation. On January 18, 1871, Bismarck took part in the greatest event of his career. In the Hall of Mirrors of Versailles Palace just outside Paris, the German Empire was proclaimed. The shrewd Prussian chancellor had to battle to the last. It took strong argument on his part to convince King William to accept the imperial crown and agree to become the first emperor, or kaiser, of Germany. Bismarck had no intention of allowing the new empire to become a loose union of German states. For almost twenty years he guided Germany in its relations with other nations and molded a new world power according to Prussian ideals.

The first few years after the Treaty of Frankfurt was signed were prosperous years. A five-billion-franc indemnity from France spurred industry. Steel production reached new highs and German shipyards created a commercial fleet that worried British merchants. German commerce, no longer shackled by the customs regulations of a multitude of independent states, grew enormously. Machines operated by steam replaced waterwheels and other outmoded devices. A land that relied upon crops grown by its peasants and crafts centered in its homes, suddenly became an industrial nation. These changes marked the dawn of an era in which new classes were created by the profits of business and the skills of men who operated machines. Now political parties demanded new rights and benefits. The problems were many, but Bismarck had determined his goals and formulated his strategy even before the Reichstag (parliament) held its first meeting in Berlin.

He branded the forces which opposed him as enemies and dealt with them ruthlessly.

The chancellor's first target was the Center party; most of its members were Catholic. This group opposed his plan to make Germany a capitalistic state, secularized, with a strong army and a centralized government. The Liberals, the strongest party in the early days of the empire, gave the support he needed to put his measures through the Reichstag. Bills passed in 1873 took from the Catholic church the political power it possesssed.

Bismarck waged war on socialism with the aid of both Liberals and the Center party. Two assassination attempts on the life of Kaiser Wilhelm in 1878 gave Bismarck sufficient support for measures aimed at suppressing socialism and curbing unions. The would-be assassins were not members of the Socialist party, but the chancellor made the most of the incidents. He also dissolved the old Reichstag, which failed to grant the power he wished, and obtained a new Reichstag that supported him.

In the strong centralized government the legislative body had little or no voice. The Liberals demanded that it have more power. They also opposed Bismarck's request for tariffs to protect German industry from foreign competition. To thwart any trend toward socialism, the chancellor initiated social reforms himself. His bills to provide health insurance and old-age benefits were passed and became law. They became the pattern for similar legislation in other lands.

The emperor and chancellor had almost unrestricted power in foreign affairs. Wilhelm left these problems entirely to Bismarck. Diplomatic moves made by the chancellor were aimed at protection from France, prevention of war between Russia and Austria, and keeping the friendship of both Great Britain and Russia. He wished to avoid any major war, so alliances were made as cautiously as moves in a game of chess. He devised a system of treaties to balance the power of the nations of Europe. In 1873, a meeting was arranged between the kaiser, Czar Alexander of Russia, and Emperor Franz Joseph of Austria-Hungary. It led to an agreement to suppress socialistic ideas through what historians have called the Three Emperors' Alliance. To Bismarck it was a step toward preventing either Russia or Austria-Hungary from becoming an ally of republican France.

The Congress of Berlin was held in 1878 to decide the fate of the Balkan countries after a war between Turkey and Russia. Turkish rule over the Slavic peoples of the region had been intolerable and Russia had warred on Turkey to put an end to it. Neither Austria nor Great Britain wanted Russia to control the Balkans. Bismarck, as president of the congress, had to face many delicate diplomatic situations. The Balkans were partitioned. Most of the settlements made were unsatsifactory to Russia.

In September, 1879, Germany signed a military alliance with Austria-Hungary that guaranteed support in case of attack by Russia. Italy joined in this agreement in 1883. It became known as the Triple Alliance. Kaiser Wilhelm objected to this secret treaty with Austria because of his great friendship for Czar Alexander, who was his nephew. The Three Emperors' Alliance expired in 1887 because Russia did not wish to renew an agreement that included Austria. But a Reinsurance Treaty was signed secretly by Russia and Germany, binding each country to refrain from entering any conflict with a major power in which the other might become involved. The treaty, however, did not apply if Russia declared war on Austria, or Germany engaged in hostilities with France.

Bismarck did not include a large colonial empire in his plans for a strong Germany. Despite his country's need of grain and certain raw materials for industry, he did not favor risking war with Great Britain or France over colonial rights. He also frowned upon the idea of having a navy larger than was needed to defend Germany's North Sea and Baltic coasts. But some territory in Africa was acquired in 1884. This was followed by the addition of more African colonies and, years later, of some island groups in the South Pacific.

Wilhelm I died March 17, 1888, at the age of ninety-one. His son, Frederick III, was ill with cancer of the throat when he ascended the throne. He reigned only ninety-nine days. In June, 1888, Frederick's son became emperor, Kaiser Wilhelm II.

Bismarck remained as chancellor during the first few years of the young emperor's reign. He found Wilhelm II quite different from his grandfather. The kaiser's insistence upon an active part in government and the right to make his own decisions led to disagreements. In 1890 the aging chancellor tendered his resignation. The kaiser accepted it and appointed General Leo von Caprivi to the post. The master statesman who had created a united Germany spent his remaining years in retirement on his estate near Friedrichsruhe. His removal marked the beginning of a new era in the history of the German Empire.

Cologne Cathedral at night. Equestrian statue of Kaiser Wilhelm II is in the foreground.

Through his system of alliances, Bismarck tried to create a balance between European powers to lessen the chances of a major war and to avoid encirclement by an anti-German coalition. Wilhelm II delighted in thrusting himself into the controversies between world powers, although it often led to blunders and hazardous situations. The emperor allowed the Reinsurance Treaty with Russia to lapse in 1891. Russia immediately looked for new allies and eventually forced Germany to defend herself on both her eastern and western fronts. Wilhelm II also failed to accept an opportunity to sign a treaty with Britain. In 1894 a Franco-Russian alliance became a reality. Years later it was broadened to include Britain and became known as the Triple Entente.

On several occasions the kaiser emphasized his determination to bring Germany into world politics. Other nations were creating alliances that surrounded Germany and Austria-Hungary with potential enemies. The Habsburg empire of Franz Joseph leaned heavily upon German support in its international relations. Austrian control of Balkan territory caused friction because of strong trends toward nationalism among the Slavs. Germany needed allies to balance the power of nations, linked by treaties, that encircled it. She developed friendly relations with Turkey, an old enemy of Russia. German capitalists planned construction of a Berlin-to-Baghdad railroad which would link Germany with the Near East. These developments aroused the suspicions of both the Russians and the British.

Admiral von Tirpitz, navy minister in Kaiser Wilhelm's official family, enlisted public opinion in his plan for a large navy. Soon German shipyards began launching dreadnoughts and submarines, thus threatening Britain's supremacy of the seas.

Shortly after an agreement had been reached with the British regarding the Berlin-to-Baghdad railroad, a tragic incident in the Balkans startled the world. On June 8, 1914, Archduke Francis Ferdinand, heir to the throne of Austria-Hungary, was assassinated. The event occurred in Sarajevo, capital of Bosnia, a Balkan region annexed to the Habsburg empire. A crazed youth influenced by a Serbian organization to promote independence fired the shots. European diplomats cut short their summer vacations. Lights burned through the night in the ministries of state and defense in Paris, Berlin, London, Vienna, St. Petersburg. Austria accused Serbian officials of a part in the plot and the kaiser sent word to Franz Joseph that Austria should decide what demands should be made on Serbia.

The situation became more serious on July 25, 1914, when Serbia's reply to the harsh Austrian ultimatum did not fully satisfy the Habsburg government. On that same day, Czar Nicholas II ordered the mobilization of the Russian army. A German note demanded that Russia cease preparations for war, but the deadline passed with no reply. Germany declared war on Russia on August 1. To meet her obligations in her Franco-Russian alliance, France issued a call to arms. Belgium refused a German request for permission to march her armies through Belgian territory in an attack on France. German troops immediately swarmed across both Belgium and Luxembourg, and this action brought a declaration of war by Britain on August 4.

World War I had begun. At the outset Russia, France, and Britain (the Allies) were the major powers aligned against Germany, Turkey, and Austria-Hungary (the Central Powers). Italy and Japan entered the conflict on the side of the Allies somewhat later and, in 1915, Bulgaria sided with the Central Powers. In April, 1917, the United States was drawn into the war after Germany launched unrestricted submarine warfare against Allied shipping. Germany was now confronted by her enemies on two fronts—Russia on her eastern borders and France, Britain, and the United States in the west. Her fleet, held in the Baltic Sea except for submarine forays, played a minor role. The kaiser, chancellor, and parliament lost their powers early in the war to General Ludendorff. He became a virtual dictator over every military and political move.

In the spring of 1918, victory came to the armies of General Paul von Hindenburg on the eastern front. He soon became the idol of the nation. Lithuania, Poland, and Ukraina were no longer under Russian rule. This was extremely advantageous to Germany since most of

Russia's coal and iron mines could now supply her industries with sorely needed materials.

A number of factors eventually led to the collapse of Russia. There was blundering and graft in her army. Her soldiers were poorly clad and hungry, and lacked ammunition. They were eager to revolt. A revolution in St. Petersburg in March, 1917, brought the abdication of Czar Nicholas II. A provisional government was set up, but its attempt to continue the war met with failure. Control then went to the Bolsheviks who established a Communist government under the leadership of Vladimir I. Lenin. The war between Russia and Germany came to an end when the Treaty of Brest-Litovsk was signed on March 3, 1918.

German hopes for victory in the west seemed to brighten by midsummer of 1918. Then a breakthrough by the British army forced General Ludendorff to make preparations for surrender. Prince Max of Baden was made chancellor and a constitutional form of government was established. Sailors of the German fleet went on strike when they learned of the plans of the admirals to sail the fleet out of Kiel for a final battle with the enemy. Kaiser Wilhelm went into exile in Holland. Finally, on November 11, 1918, an armistice agreement was signed that ended hostilities.

In June, 1919, German representatives came to the Hall of Mirrors at Versailles to sign the peace treaty. The ceremony contrasted sharply with the event which had taken place there in 1871 when Bismarck's dream of a united Germany was realized. The treaty ceded Alsace-Lorraine and the Saar, with its rich coal deposits, to France. Also, upon the insistence of France, Germany was required to pay a huge indemnity. A "war guilt" clause which branded the German nation as the power responsible for the war was included.

The German people, though their representatives signed the treaty offered to them in the Hall of Mirrors, did not see the document as an instrument to guarantee peace. They bitterly assailed its terms. The German empire was gone; replaced by a republic. German leaders turned their attention to the task of reconstruction.

# 7

## Republic, Dictatorship, and Collapse

After her surrender in 1918, Germany faltered toward recovery. The postwar years were hectic. The country was ready for unrest; the harsh and humiliating terms of the peace treaty caused bitterness and anger. German unity was cracking under the strain of hunger, inflation, and defeat.

The Paris conferences in 1919 and 1920 sought a formula for permanent peace. It was there that President Woodrow Wilson's dream of a world organization to prevent war became a reality in the League of Nations. But Wilson's achievements at the peace conference received a mixed reception in his own country. Isolationism was strong in America. The United States Senate refused to ratify the Versailles Treaty and to participate in the League of Nations. A separate treaty between Germany and the United States ended the state of war.

In November, 1918, after the abdication of the Hohenzollern monarch, Prince Max of Baden gave the reins of government to Friedrich Ebert, a leader of the majority branch of the Social Democratic party. Revolts by sailors and workers occurred in the big cities. Fighting broke out in Berlin. The Spartacists, a radical group, appealed to the workers to overthrow the Ebert government and set up a dictatorship of the workers, as in Russia. To cope with these uprisings, the provisional government called remnants of the old army to its aid.

The National Assembly met in Weimar in February, 1919. After months of deliberation it drew up a constitution for the German republic, to be headed by a president and a chancellor. The chancellor of the republic would be dependent upon both the president and the Reichstag and could be forced by either to resign. The new government was commonly called the Weimar Republic. Friedrich Ebert was elected president by the National Assembly on February 11, 1919.

A large proportion of the German people, knowing only the ways of a monarchy, had little confidence in the new form of government. Many blamed the republic for the Treaty of Versailles, although it had no part in shaping the terms. In the shuffling of old political divisions to form new units called *Laender,* regional differences were roused. It was also blamed for the wild inflation that sent the value of the mark plummeting. In 1923, the mark reached a low of over four billion to the dollar.

Plots to overthrow the republic, internal strife, and assassinations were common in the early years of the era. In the spring of 1920 army officers joined monarchists in an attempt to seize control. Their leaders included Wolfgang Kapp and General Ludendorff. The Kapp *Putsch* (plot) was not a success. Walter Rathenau, minister of foreign affairs in 1922, aroused the enmity of several factions. His policy of fulfillment of treaty obligations brought improved conditions. He also brought about an agreement with Russia for mutual cancellation of reparations claims between the two countries in the Treaty of Rapallo (April, 1922). On June 24, 1922, Rathenau was assassinated by youths believed to have been supported by Nationalists.

German passive resistance tactics in the delivery of materials for reparations brought French troops into the Ruhr in 1923. There was mass unemployment and inflation. Not until Gustav Stresemann became chancellor in that same year was progress made again toward recovery and stabilization. Stresemann convinced the Allies that reparations requirements were stifling recovery. This led to the Dawes Plan, accepted by Germany in 1924, which specified definite annual payments.

Field Marshal Paul von Hindenburg, popular because of the victories of his armies on the eastern front, became president in 1925. The very capable Gustav Stresemann was his minister of foreign affairs. The Locarno Pact, a series of treaties guaranteeing frontiers and agreeing to arbitration as a means of settling disputes, was signed in 1925. The Young Plan, adopted in 1929, set the total reparations bill at nearly twenty-nine billion dollars to be paid over a period of almost sixty years.

Germany, like other nations of Europe, was caught in the world depression following the New York Stock Exchange crash in 1929. Unrest and unemployment grew and the activities of political agitators increased. A conference in Lausanne, Switzerland, in 1932 brought an end to reparations payments.

President Hindenburg was reelected in April, 1932, and a few weeks later Chancellor Bruening was dismissed. Franz von Papen was appointed by the president to fill the post but proved so unsatisfactory that he was soon replaced by General Kurt von Schleicher.

Political scheming flourished among the advisors of President Hindenburg and there were many cliques with selfish motives. One included army officers who opposed the republican form of government. Another was a group of industrialists who had fared well during the period of inflation. This latter group influenced Hindenburg to remove Schleicher and appoint Adolf Hitler, whose national Socialist (Nazi) party had gained many seats in the Reichstag.

Born in Austria in 1889, Hitler was the son of a customs officer in the border town of Braunau. He had ambitions to become an artist and applied to a Vienna art school for admission but was refused because he did not show enough talent. Discouraged, he went to Munich and volunteered for service in the German army in World War I. After the war he returned to Munich and founded a small political group—the National Socialist party.

An attempt was made in November, 1923, to overthrow the government. Adolf Hitler and General Erich Ludendorff were the leaders. This was the first National Socialist revolt, more commonly known as the Munich Beer Hall Putsch. Hitler was sent to Landsberg Prison for a five-year sentence, but was released after serving six months. In prison, with the help of Rudolf Hess, a fellow prisoner, he wrote *Mein Kampf.* The book presented the strange philosophy which became the basis of Nazi policies and strategy.

At the end of World War I no one would have thought the brooding, lonely Adolf Hitler, unable to rise above the rank of corporal, was destined to rule Germany. No one would have dreamed that within a couple of decades he would make the decisions and give the orders that would change the map of Europe, send millions to their death, and wreak vengeance on those who opposed him. He looked upon treaties as promises to be broken. His philosophy became the core of the Nazi movement. A major aim was to give leadership in Germany to members of the Nordic race. These were the fair-haired, blue-eyed Germans found most frequently in just a few areas of northern Germany. Since the number of pure Nordics was small, the idea of a superior race was broadened to include all Germans. They were called Aryans. Jews were excluded. Hitler had an intense hatred of Jews. They became the scapegoats of the Nazis and were brutally persecuted. Hitler believed that whoever could obtain control of central Europe would control the world.

Shortly after he left prison Hitler's meteoric rise to power began. Conditions were ripe for revolt. In the thirties more than nine million Germans were unemployed and industrial production had slowed dangerously. The people blamed the country's economic ills on the terms of the Treaty of Versailles. They resented the burden of reparations in retaliation for the destruction Germany had caused in the war. Demilitarizing of the Rhineland, the loss of colonies, and the crippling of the economy embittered them further. Hitler, talented in demagogic oratory, fanned the flames of hatred to win votes for his party.

As the National Socialist party gained strength the SA and the SS were organized. The SA were the storm troops (*Sturmableitung*) or Brown Shirts, founded by Hermann Goering to guard Nazi speakers. The SS (*Schutzstaffeln*) or Black Shirts were Hitler's personal bodyguard; each member pledged to give his life, if necessary, for his leader. Nazi rabble-rousers ranted about communism, the "slave treaty" (Treaty of Versailles), the party in power, and the Jews.

Hindenburg appointed Hitler to the chancellorship in January, 1933. The votes of fourteen million Germans in the elections of 1932 had given the Nazis a majority in the Reichstag. As a result, their leader became chancellor.

Hitler had vowed he would rid the country of Jews. Less than four months after he became chancellor, all Jews were removed from positions in government and the faculties of universities, and were forbidden to enter the professions. They were required to wear a badge, the Star of David, at all times for identification. A law prohibited marriage between Jews and persons of "German blood." Their shops were picketed. The terror to which these people were subjected, however, did not reach its peak until the outbreak of the war in 1939. Then the tempo of Gestapo activities increased. The Gestapo were the state police, organized in 1933 when Germany became a police state, and became the spy system which operated throughout the land. They rounded up Jews for removal to concentration camps after their property was confiscated. Others who, though not Jews, were openly opposed to Nazism, were given like treatment. They were shipped like cattle—men, women, and children—to extermination centers.

Thousands who were poorly fed or starved or suffering from disease were worked to death or shot when they dropped exhausted from overexertion. Others were herded into the gas chambers of the extermination centers and killed. Then their bodies were burned in crematories operated in conjunction with these chambers of horror. Many such extermination centers were operating throughout this period in Germany and in invaded countries under Nazi control. One was Auschwitz, a short distance from Cracow, Poland. Another was Dachau, not far from Munich. Others included Buchenwald, Treblinka, Belsen, and many more. Members of the SS and the Gestapo served as guards in some of these. As far as possible their purpose was kept secret. It has been claimed that at Auschwitz alone nearly four million were put to death.

The horrors of the extermination centers were revealed to all Germans after the armies of the Allies occupied the country. They were required to attend showings of pictures that proved what terrible crimes and mass murders had been committed. War crimes trials led to prison terms or death penalties for hundreds proven guilty. The trials held at Nuremburg attracted the most attention because so many of the Nazi leaders were among those being tried. Since the war the extermination center at Dachau has become an historic site so that visitors may see for themselves and learn to what depths the minds of those who perpetrated the crimes had sunk.

After the death of the aged President Hindenburg in 1934, Hitler took over the presidency and combined it with his position as chancellor under the title of *Fuehrer* (leader). The Reichstag was dissolved to give him a free hand in shaping and carrying out his program for making Germany self-sufficient, bringing under one flag all areas occupied by Germans, and, by expanding to the east, creating the *Lebensraum* (living space) his *Grossdeutschland* (Greater Germany) would require. In October, 1933, Hitler notified the League of Nations that Germany would be rearmed and conscription would be resumed to build up her armed forces. In 1936 he sent his troops into the Rhineland, a part of Germany which was supposed to remain demilitarized according to peace treaty terms. The action brought little more than formal protests from the great powers. More than eighteen billion marks were budgeted for rearmament in 1938. This reduced unemployment to half a million and also raised living standards in Germany. In the summer of 1936 German troops and weapons were sent into the civil war in Spain to help the Fascist insurgents who were receiving similar help from Italy. Russia was providing troops and equipment for the opposite side in this war, the Loyalists. Germany's motive was to provide her soldiers with battle experience and to test out military techniques and weapons. On the home front Germany was rapidly becoming a police state. Every trick of the propagandist and gangster was used in domestic affairs. Wealthy industrialists, who had contributed generously to the Nazi movement in an effort to overthrow the republic but who now hoped to rid themselves of Hitler after he had served his purpose, found themselves outmaneuvered. To indoctrinate young Germans with Nazi ideals, Hitler Youth Groups were formed in the large cities and towns.

The Fuehrer's first target beyond the borders of Germany was his native Austria where Nazi organizations within the borders were already attempting to undermine the government. For several years they had been working toward *Anschluss* (union) with Germany. With Hitler's help they attempted to overthrow the Austrian regime in 1934. The Austrian chancellor, Engelbert Dollfuss, was assassinated. But his successor, Kurt von Schuschnigg, kept the country independent a few more years. Finally, in the spring of 1938, the German army swept across the border and Austria became a part of Germany. Great Britain sent Hitler a protest. The Fuehrer did not bother to answer.

Hitler's next target in his drive for territory was Czechoslovakia, a land formed by the treaty-makers in 1918 from Moravia, Bohemia, Slovakia, and Ruthenia, and including the German-populated Sudetenland. He put pressure upon the Czechs to return the Sudetenland to Germany. Neville Chamberlain of Great Britain and Edouard Daladier of France met with Hitler in Munich in the autumn of 1938 in an attempt to appease him. A direct result of this meeting was the Munich Pact which provided for the dismemberment of Czechoslovakia. In March, 1939, Hitler sent his troops into that country. The Sudetenland became German territory again, and Moravia and Bohemia, German protectorates.

The intentions of the Fuehrer became clear. The appeasers knew the next target would be Poland. The Nazis had not only taken over Czechoslovakia, but also captured Lithuania's chief port, the city of Memel. Hitler then renounced the nonaggression treaty with Poland. Great Britain and France signed a mutual assistance treaty with Poland in April, 1939. Hitler demanded that Poland surrender the Polish Corridor—the territory between East Prussia and the rest of Germany. The Soviets had been negotiating with the French and British for an alliance against Germany. Before an agreement was reached it was learned that Germany and Russia had signed a secret nonaggression pact to conquer Poland and to divide the country between them.

September 1, 1939, was the fateful day that ushered in World War II. Hitler ordered his armed forces to strike with lightning speed. Mechanized infantry led by the tanks of panzer divisions crossed the Polish border from East Prussia. Simultaneously another of his armies attacked from the southeast, headed toward Warsaw, the capital of Poland. Within a few days the small Polish army, mainly cavalry, was destroyed. Poland's air force of eight hundred outmoded planes was no match for the more than six thousand planes of the German Luftwaffe that streaked across the sky above the Polish plains. They machine-gunned the peasants who clogged the roads in their flight from burning villages. Neither the British nor the French had time to come to Poland's aid, although both had declared war on Germany a day or two after the Nazis struck. This was a new kind of war that became known as a *Blitzkrieg* (lightning war). German and Soviet armies met at Brest-Litovsk and on September 27 the two aggressors signed the treaty that partitioned Poland between them. The beautiful city of Warsaw had been reduced to smoldering, blackened ruins. Thousands of Poles were sent to extermination centers and thousands more were deported to Germany and Siberia to work as slave laborers. Hitler had taken the Polish Corridor in one of the shortest, most terrible campaigns in military history!

On the western front, hostilities developed slowly over a period of many months. The French army waited behind the fortified Maginot Line near the Franco-German border. The German armies were poised behind their Siegfried Line. But Nazi strategists decided to carry the war to the high seas. Both the British and the French were superior to Germany in naval power, except for her submarines. The British blockaded the entrance to the Baltic Sea to bottle up most of the ships of the German fleet. Despite the blockade, a "pocket battleship" or two, like the *Admiral Graf Spee,* escaped to take their toll of Allied ships. Nazi submarines preyed upon merchantmen and scuttled some Allied naval vessels in British ports. About this time the government of Neville Chamberlain received a vote of no confidence in the British Parliament. Sir Winston Churchill succeeded him as prime minister. Churchill's persistent determination to defeat the Nazis, despite the hardships and discouragements to which the people of Britain were subjected in the early years of the war, contributed much toward final victory.

After the occupation and partition of Poland, Nazi leaders focused their attention on the Scandinavian countries. German industry was dependent upon high-grade iron ore from Sweden and nickel from Finland for the manufacture of guns, tanks, and other war equipment. The British had mined the waters off the Norwegian coast to prevent a German invasion of that country. But hundreds of German ships, protected from enemy attack by the planes of the Luftwaffe, eventually managed to land troops in Norwegian ports and occupy the country. German troops also converged on Denmark. The small, poorly trained Danish army offered little resistance. Within a few days Denmark was occupied.

The Low Countries, Belgium and the Netherlands, were the next invasion target of the Nazis. Early on the morning of April 9, 1940, hundreds of German airplanes appeared in the skies over the Netherlands. They dropped paratroopers behind the Dutch lines and dive-bombers screamed toward towns and villages. The Dutch army was too small to cope with the German invasion forces which crossed their borders. The lowlands were flooded by opening the dikes in a vain attempt to halt the Germans. The Luftwaffe attacked Rotterdam and reduced the heart of the city to a mass of rubble. The Hague also was attacked. Amsterdam was saved from a similar fate when the general commanding the city's defenses saw the futility of resisting and decided to surrender. Queen Wilhelmina and high government officials escaped to England on a British destroyer to set up a government in exile in London. Large stocks of gold and diamonds were also carried to London on British vessels so they would not fall into the hands of the Nazis.

German forces, after the Netherlands had been taken, converged on Belgium. Belgian resistance was strong initially, but with the fall of Antwerp and Brussels, Belgium surrendered. French generals tried in vain to hold back the invading German army but it fought its way through the Maginot Line. French troops were routed, villages were destroyed. A large number of German divisions were ordered to move toward the French coast to annihilate British, French, and Dutch troops attempting to reach Dunkirk on the English Channel. Dunkirk had been selected as the port of evacuation. Thousands waiting on the beaches were strafed by German planes. The hundreds of vessels of all types that shuttled back and forth across the channel were able to rescue less than a third of the encircled troops and get them safely to the English coast.

German generals sent planes, tanks, and mechanized troops against the demoralized French forces. Hostilities broke out in the east where Mussolini ordered his troops, massed along the Franco-Italian frontier, to strike to weaken the defenses of the French in the west. Paris was declared an open city to save it from destruction. Premier Paul Renaud resigned. Marshal Henri Philippe Pétain, his successor, asked for and was granted an armistice. French and German officials met in a railway coach on June 22, 1940, to arrange the terms. This was the same spot where almost two decades before the Germans had the same humiliating experience of accepting the armistice terms dictated by the victors in World War I. Northern and central France was occupied and the French government set up Vichy as its capital. The Free French, under the leadership of Charles de Gaulle, set up their capital in London to work toward liberating their country.

The Battle of Britain began on July 10, 1940, when squadrons of German planes appeared over London, bombed the heart of the city, and then continued their raids on the capital day after day. An invasion of the British Isles appeared imminent. Barges and landing craft had been accumulated in ports along the French, Dutch, and Belgian coasts, and troops were concentrated in the area. Nazi submarines and planes set up a blockade of British ports in an attempt to prevent supplies from reaching England. Although Britain's Royal Air Force was no match for the Luftwaffe, the Germans had underestimated the determination of the British under the leadership of Prime Minister Churchill. Air raids were intensified during the winter months, with London and important industrial centers as the targets. London was severely damaged and Coventry was left in ruins from night raids during which incendiary bombs were dropped. In retaliation RAF planes destroyed large areas of Bremen and attacked coastal cities on the Continent where Nazi troops awaited orders to cross the channel. Throughout the winter the British, half-starved and short of fuel, worked furiously to prepare defenses for the expected attack. By March, 1941, convoys of ships loaded with food, guns, ammunition, and other supplies provided through the Lend-Lease Act passed by the United States Congress, began to arrive. Increase in the strength of the RAF and in the aid flowing to England from the United States gave Hitler second thoughts about invading Britain. A decision made by Italy (with Japan, Germany's leading Axis partner) quickly turned the attention of the Fuehrer away from Britain. Mussolini decided to conquer Greece. Although his armies won some initial successes, the Greeks, supported by British troops and planes, drove the invaders back across the borders of the country and pursued them through the mountain passes of Albania. To settle the debacle Mussolini had precipitated, the Germans invaded Yugoslavia and drove the British out of Greece. Nazi strategists realized that Crete had become an island outpost of the British in the eastern Mediterranean. The Luftwaffe's bombers, transport planes, and gliders attacked Crete and brought in troops. Paratroopers were dropped on the island, the defenders of the island were defeated, and the island was occupied by the Germans.

The war had by now become a global conflict. Japan, overconfident because of a successful campaign in Manchuria, clashed with Soviet troops on the Siberian frontier. These incidents and the movement of

German troops into the Balkans were viewed as serious threats to the Soviet Union. However, the Soviets settled their differences with Japan in April, 1941, and signed a nonaggression pact with that nation. Fighting spread to many areas, including other parts of the Balkans, the colonial empire of Italy in Africa, Egypt, and Iran. One of Hitler's objectives was to drive the British out of the Mediterranean and make it a Nazi sea. But British victories in Africa over Italian forces and Germany's Afrika Korps, under the command of Field Marshal Erwin Rommel (1891–1944), put an end to the Fuehrer's hopes.

On June 22, 1941, German troops crossed the western borders of the Soviet Union along a two-thousand-mile-front. Joseph Stalin, the Soviet premier, had joined the Allied powers shortly before. Germany prepared for what her military strategists called Operation Barbarossa. Hitler's goal was the capture of Moscow and Leningrad and the occupation of the industrial centers in the Ural Mountains, the great grain-producing centers of the Ukraine, and the rich oil deposits of the Caucasus region. This would also make the Volga a German river.

The German war machine and industrial production were still strong. Civilians from the occupied countries became slave laborers for the Nazis. Jews in many areas were ferreted out and sent to concentration camps or extermination centers. Where pockets of resistance were found, entire villages were destroyed, and in some the inhabitants were shot.

As the German armies rushed across the western borders, the Soviet dictator demanded that his people destroy their crops and stores of grain and drive out their cattle. Hitler sent nearly three million men and thousands of tanks into the battle. The Red Army reeled under the crushing blow. Several squadrons of the best Nazi planes strafed and bombed in advance of the invading armies. Russians taken prisoner were sent to Germany or the occupied countries for forced labor. The "scorched earth" policy Stalin demanded of his people was not carried out in many areas. The inhabitants of some Soviet villages welcomed the invaders. They felt Stalin was a ruthless dictator and

hoped that life under Hitler might be better. They were disappointed
—they were forced to work like slaves for the Germans, and some were
put to death. Most were ill-treated. Friendliness on the part of the
Russian peasants soon turned to hatred. Aid came to the Soviets in
July, 1941, through an agreement with the British signed in Moscow.
Iran was occupied by Soviet and British troops to provide a supply
route into the Soviet Union. Rostov, Kiev, other important Russian
cities, and the Crimea were in German hands. The Nazis were on the
threshold of Moscow in October, only thirty miles from the city. When
the severe winter weather began in November, the Russians gathered
enough strength to launch a strong counterattack. The Germans re-
treated and gave up some of the cities they had taken, including Rostov. Although they had failed to take Moscow, they held vast areas of
western Russia. In the early part of June, 1942, they launched an
offensive. Rostov and much of the Caucasus were retaken. Other German armies far to the north advanced toward Stalingrad. Nazi air attacks reduced much of the city to ruins before it was captured. But in
February, 1943, the Soviets encircled the Germans and forced them to
surrender.

The war in Asia had expanded on December 7, 1941, when Japanese planes made a sneak attack on Pearl Harbor and destroyed most
of the United States Pacific Fleet. The United States declared war on
Japan and on her allies, Germany and Italy. The war in the Pacific
was separate from the conflict raging in Europe. Neither Germany nor
Italy was directly involved. American forces, however, now took a
major role in the battles in Europe and northern Africa.

Rommel's Afrika Korps was surrounded on Cape Bon in Tunisia
and forced to surrender to the Americans and British in the summer of
1943. Then northern Africa became a training area for an invasion of
Nazi-held Europe.

Troops of the Allies invaded Sicily early in July, 1943, and occupied
the island. British and American troops then gained a foothold on the
Italian peninsula. The Italians, tired of fascism, war, and Mussolini,
overthrew their government, and the new government offered to join

the Allies. The strong resistance of German forces still in possession of strategic points along the peninsula made conquest of Italy a slow and difficult operation. But when Rome fell in June, 1944, the Germans withdrew. With Italy on the side of the Allies and the German armies driven northward, the United States Air Force and the RAF were soon bombing cities in Germany.

France was invaded on June 6, 1944, during one of the most massive, and well-planned operations in military history. American General Dwight Eisenhower was in command of the huge army that crossed the English Channel in the early hours of the morning to land on the beaches of Normandy. About four thousand ships and more than ten thousand planes carried the men and equipment of the invading force that fought its way into the interior of France. Somewhat later another huge invasion force, assembled in Italy and North Africa, entered southern France and moved northward. Paris was liberated in August and by September several armies of the Allies had reached the borders of Germany. Cities of the Rhineland, the Ruhr valley, and northern Germany were soon being bombed. One of the last big battles of the war along the western front was fought in December, 1944, when the Germans launched a counteroffensive through the Ardennes Forest in an attempt to reach Antwerp. This was the Battle of the Bulge.

The Red Army, fighting in the east, the Balkans, the Ukraine, and Poland, drove the Germans from most of the territory they had occupied, with tremendous losses in men, planes, and tanks. By January, 1945, the Soviets had penetrated eastern Germany and were on their way to Berlin. They entered the city in late April. Allied troops had crossed the Rhine and were capturing cities in the heart of Germany.

On May 7, 1945, Germany accepted the Allies' terms of unconditional surrender. Hitler, who had dreamed of creating a *Grossdeutschland* and dominating Europe, ended his life by committing suicide in the bunker of his headquarters in Berlin on April 30, 1945.

On the other side of the world the war in the Pacific continued until late summer. On August 6, 1945, the first atomic bomb used in war was dropped on Hiroshima. A few days later the Soviet Union declared war on Japan and drove Japanese troops out of Manchuria. Japan surrendered on August 14, 1945.

The world paid an enormous price for the war that began when Adolf Hitler ordered his troops into Poland on September 1, 1939. The cost in dollars to the nations taking part in this conflict cannot be accurately estimated. And who can even begin to measure the cost in terms of the millions who lost their lives, and millions more who still bear the scars?

# 8

## The Laender of West Germany

The Federal Republic of Germany (West Germany) is divided into ten states or *Laender*. Each *Land* has a legislature, a cabinet of ministers, and a president. The office of *Land* president corresponds to that of governor in our states. Each *Land* also has several broad powers such as the right to tax, to shape its cultural policies and educational system, and to maintain police. The ten laender are Baden-Wuerttemberg, Bavaria, Bremen, Hamburg, Hesse, Lower Saxony, North Rhine-Westphalia, Rhineland-Palatinate, Saarland, and Schleswig-Holstein. West Berlin has *Land* status also, but it is inoperative because of the occupation agreement of 1945.

### BAVARIA

Bavarians, a pleasure-loving and hospitable people, are proud to share the natural beauty of the Alps along the southern border of their *Land* with the throngs of visitors who come from all parts of Europe and from overseas. An excellent system of trails leads through the forests, across high meadows and into rugged mountain terrain. Hikers using these trails can reach vantage points overlooking quiet valleys and alpine lakes. When glistening snow mantles the valleys and the slopes of jagged peaks, skiers flock to the mountain resorts. On many a winter evening village folk go to their favorite inn after chores are done to enjoy zither music and join in songs and laughter over a stein of beer. This mountain country is also the home of woodcarvers, vio-

71

lin-makers, foresters, and farmers. In early autumn Munich, the capital and largest city, becomes the holiday center of Bavaria during the annual Oktoberfest. Again in the days before Lent, when Faschingtime arrives and the carnival fun is at its peak, rural folk come to Munich. In the large cities Sunday mass is held in impressive cathedrals where worshippers have come for centuries. In country communities many Bavarians wear their colorful folk costumes and walk to a little church with its tower crowned by an "onion bulb" top, characteristic of churches of the region.

Bavaria today is Germany's largest *Land,* about three times the area of Massachusetts. The Danube River, which rises in the Black Forest of neighboring Baden-Wuerttemberg, flows across it from west to east. That part of Bavaria north of the Danube is known as Franconia, a region of more ancient cities, many historic walled towns and castles, and fields of grain. Here are Nuremberg, where toymaking is a major industry; Bamberg, once ruled by a powerful bishop who became Pope Clement II; and Bayreuth, where the operas of Richard Wagner are presented in the Festspielhaus, built in 1876. Bavarians living in central Franconia are mostly Catholic. In other areas they are pre-

A young lady in a Bavarian folk costume.

dominantly Protestant. The region south of the Danube which surrounds Munich is called Upper Bavaria or Ober-Bayern.

The Alps, which form a high wall of jagged peaks shared with Austria, consist of several ranges within Bavarian territory. The Allgaeu Alps are to the west. The Wetterstein and Karwendel mountains with Germany's highest peak, the Zugspitze (9,721 feet), are in the central part. The Berchtesgadner Alps with the Koenigsee, one of the most beautiful lakes in Germany, are to the east. Alpine roses and edelweiss thrive in the rock crevices of the high peaks in summer. Glacial meltwater forms raging streams that become waterfalls in their plunge from rock ledges. Red deer graze in meadows where mountain violets and alpine poppies bloom. The entire region is a paradise for hikers, hunters, and skiers.

Almost four centures ago pestilence fell upon the village of Oberammergau when the Black Death invaded central Europe. The villagers prayed for relief and vowed that if their prayers were answered they would present a pageant at regular intervals depicting the suffering and death of Christ. In keeping with that promise the Passion Play has been produced during the summer months of every tenth year since 1634, almost without interruption. In recent years the play has been presented in the huge new open-air Passion Play Theater. The actors are chosen from among the residents of Oberammergau.

In the mountainous areas of Bavaria, particularly in the Alps, there has been a revival of the use of fresco painting in decorating the exterior walls of buildings—a technique developed centuries ago. Bavarian artists use watercolors to paint life-size historical, legendary, or religious scenes on the plaster surface of outside walls of homes, shops, and inns. The colors combine chemically with the plaster to become so permanent that sun, rain, and freezing weather have no effect upon them.

Garmisch-Partenkirchen, commonly called simply Garmisch, is one of the world's best-known mountain resorts. It lies high in the Alps between Mittenwald and Oberammergau and is ideally situated on level ground. When skiing became a popular winter sport, attention was drawn to this tiny alpine village where snow fell early in autumn and lasted late in spring. Plenty of sunshine on winter days and the construction of a skiing and ice-skating stadium for the Winter Olympic Games in 1936 increased its popularity. Today it is much larger and busier and has many additional sports facilities including chairlifts, bobsled runs, cogwheel railways, and toboggan slides.

About A.D. 1200, southern Bavaria was granted to members of the house of Wittelsbach and ruled by dukes and kings of the Wittelsbach line until the end of World War I. In 1864 a handsome eighteen-year-old prince came to the throne as King Ludwig II. He was a melancholy, dreamy young man who cared more for music and art than for affairs of state and government. The compositions of that great musical genius, Richard Wagner, held the king spellbound, especially the operas *Lohengrin* and *Tannhaeuser*. When Ludwig became king he summoned Wagner to Munich and expressed admiration for his work. In the years that followed Ludwig financed the presentation of some of Wagner's operas, and paid his debts. With the help of his royal benefactor, the genius of the composer of such masterpieces as *Die Meistersinger von Nurnberg* and *Der Ring des Nibelungen* was recognized throughout the world.

King Ludwig also spent lavishly in building some of Germany's most beautiful castles. The first was Neuschwanstein, a fairytale castle on a rugged mountaintop commanding a spectacular view across the foothills of the Alps and the Alpsee, a picturesque lake not far from the little town of Fuessen. Within sight of it was Hohenschwangau, the castle where he had spent much of his childhood. Another, Herrenchiemsee Castle, was built on an island in a beautiful lake. During the summer, concerts are now held in its great hall illuminated by the soft light of thousands of candles. Another of his *Koenigsschloesser* (King's Castles), built in a valley not far from Munich, is Linderhof and its famous fountain in a beautiful formal garden. At regular intervals the fountain reaches a height of over one hundred feet and then subsides until time for another spectacular display. All three of these castles are now the property of the Bavarian state and are maintained for the enjoyment of the public. Eventually King Ludwig's reckless spending and his lack of interest in everything except opera and castles led to his being declared mentally unfit to rule. He was taken to Schloss Burg, a small castle on a lake, where he was to remain with his doctor. Within a few hours after his arrival, the bodies of both men were found in the lake. Both had drowned.

Munich, the Bavarian capital, is built on a plain cut by the Isar River on its way to join the Danube to the northeast. The southern limits of the city are less than fifty miles from the foothills of the Alps. Munich began to grow in 1158 primarily because Henry the Lion, duke of Bavaria and Saxony, was irked by the unscrupulous activities of a bishop. The bishop had built a much-needed bridge across the Isar River along a major trade route and he exacted an exorbitant toll from those who used it. The duke was so angry he had his men burn the bridge and then built another not far from where a group of monks had established a settlement. This was the beginning of the city of Munich. Today the coat of arms of Munich reminds us of its humble origin by depicting a monk with an open Bible in his hands.

Munich's location on both north-south and east-west trade routes contributed to its rapid growth. From its modest beginning, it has grown to have a population of more than one and a quarter million people. Now, instead of one bridge across the Isar it has sixteen. It suffered severely during both world wars. At the end of World War II most of it was a mass of rubble since it had been the target of numerous bombing missions. Many of its historic buildings were in ruins. Today the rubble has been removed and old historic structures restored, and industry and trade have made it a thriving metropolis again. Its parks, churches, and streets flanked by imposing buildings, museums, and art galleries have helped it become one of the major cultural centers of Germany. Busy squares with monuments and fountains, the medieval city gates repaired or reconstructed and the green belt of the English gardens contribute to its beauty. Each morning when the hands of the clock on the tower of the new town hall approach eleven, visitors are waiting in the Marienplatz, the square that

Munich's Marienplatz—the ornate single-towered building is the town hall. Frauenkirche is seen in the background.

is the center of the city, to enjoy the *Glockenspiel*. Figures on the tower below the clock go into action. Knights on horseback move about to simulate the action in a medieval tournament when the bells of the carillon begin to ring. Figures in colorful costumes pop out of doorways and a group of coopers dance to tunes which have been cherished for centuries. Beyond Marienplatz, which is the site of the original monks' settlement, the twin red brick towers of the Frauenkirche with their domed tops loom against the sky. This church, commonly used as a symbol of Munich, was severely damaged by bombs dropped during World War II. During the postwar period it has been completely restored. Of the city's many churches, some baroque and others rococo in architectural style, the Church of St. Peter, just a few yards away from Marienplatz, is the oldest. Other landmarks in this central area, known as Old Munich, are the busy marketplace and the Hofbrauhaus, the famous beer hall constructed during the reign of Duke William V in the sixteenth century. Until recently, brewing beer was Munich's major industry.

Munich has long attracted artists. They can be seen almost any day sketching or painting in some part of the city. Most of them live in the Schwabing quarter of the city. Art in all its forms has been encouraged. Some of the world's priceless paintings and sculptures are among the treasures stored and displayed in its art galleries and museums. The *Alte Pinakothek* (Old Painters' Gallery) has on exhibit such treasures as Rembrandt's self-portrait, Duerer's *Four Apostles,* and works of other masters of the fourteenth to sixteenth centuries.

Another important Bavarian city lies about sixty miles northwest of Munich. It is Augsburg with a population of about a quarter of a million people. In the fifteenth and sixteenth centuries Augsburg was considered one of the richest cities in Europe. Some of the homes of its well-to-do burghers still flank narrow streets in the older parts of the town. Two Augsburg families of merchant princes were extremely wealthy—the Fuggers and the Welsers. The Fuggers were originally weavers of textiles and the industry they built up is one of the most important in the city today. The Welsers, during the period in which they lived, owned most of Venezuela. Augsburg also has the distinction of providing the world's first housing project for the aid of impoverished but deserving families. Homes are rented to such families for less than a dollar a year. Operas are presented during the warm nights in summer just outside the Red Gate of the city's medieval wall. Augsburg is the largest city along what is called the "Romantic Highway"—a road that follows an ancient trade route linking several thousand-year-old towns.

The Romantic Highway begins in the south at Fuessen, not far from Neuschwanstein Castle. From Fuessen the highway extends northward, paralleling the Lech, passes through Augsburg, and a short distance west of where the river joins the Danube it reaches the picturesque medieval town of Donauwoerth. It then continues northward to several other well-preserved medieval towns. Walls built hundreds of years ago, with turrets and watchtowers that offered some security from attack by enemy forces, still remain intact in many of these towns. Streets are narrow and gilded wrought iron signs hang like pendants at the entrances to inns and the shops of craftsmen and apothecaries. Boxes on the window ledges of gabled houses brim with the blossoms of red and pink geraniums, matching the color of others that grow in medieval fountains.

Nuremberg was known as one of the finest examples of an imperial free city of the Middle Ages. During World War II lethal cargoes of bombers destroyed much of old Nuremberg in raiding missions. In the postwar period, however, most of the historic buildings have been reconstructed, and Nuremberg, sprawling over the banks of the Pegnitz River, has risen from the debris and become a fascinating city again. It has also expanded its major industry of toymaking and added many that are new, like the manufacture of electrical and electronic equipment, clothing, and furniture. Nearly half a million people live in Nuremberg today. The walk atop the city's walls, the castle on the cliff above the town, the house where Albrecht Duerer lived, and the medieval churches help visitors to picture the city as it was in earlier times.

A gilded wrought iron sign hanging above a shop entrance in Rothenburg. The main street of this medieval city appears today much as it did centuries ago.

On summer evenings old historic buildings are floodlit and in December the *Chriskindlmarkt* (Christmas Market), with its toys and Christmas tree decorations on display, is set up in the square before the Frauenkirche, one of the city's famous old churches.

Although recent years have brought new industries to the cities of all parts of Bavaria, agriculture is still a major interest. Farms in southern Bavaria are large. This is due to a law of the *Land* which requires that the eldest son be the sole heir to his father's land. In many other parts of Germany, upon a farmer's death his land is divided equally between each of the sons in his family. Homes on the farms and in the forests of southern Bavaria are solidly built. Since a large proportion of the population is Catholic, a corner of the living room is set aside for a family shrine, the *Herrgottswinkel,* usually a figure or a crucifix carved from wood and hung from the wall. Shrines can quite often be found at the side of a road or in the foothills of southern Bavaria.

Bavarian meals are substantial. The *Knoedel* (dumpling or noodle) has more or less taken the place of boiled or mashed potatoes so extensively used in other parts of Germany. Roast pork, smoked pork, and leg of veal are usually served with sauerkraut. In northern Bavaria pork sausages are popular. *Lebkuchen,* so popular during the Christmas season, originated in Nuremberg.

Although the typical regional folk costumes are not so commonly seen as they were several decades ago, there are occasions when they are worn. The folk costume of Bavarian men is quite appropriate in a land of forests and farms. Both the hat and jacket are made of *Loden,* a closely woven wool cloth that is both coldproof and waterproof and comes in shades of forest green. A brushlike ornament called the *Gamsbart* (goat's beard) is worn in the band of the hat. Wide coat lapels bear oak leaf ornaments. Coat buttons are made from deer horn. In summer short leather pants (*Lederhosen*) are worn.

## BADEN-WUERTTEMBERG

Forests, low mountain ranges, and many quaint villages tucked in the valleys that lie between them, are characteristic of the *Land* called Baden-Wuerttemberg. In the Black Forest (*Schwarzwald*) region some of the farmers and their families still live in huge brooding thatched-roofed houses that are found in no other part of Germany. The family and the farm animals are sheltered by the same gray roof of thatch. Where the *Land* reaches the shore of Lake Constance (Bodensee), the coming of spring creates a pattern of cherry orchards in blossom. In this part of the nation the winter is relatively mild. The ravines in the forests, the caves, and the quiet nooks of the mountain slopes have, through fantasy, become the abode of elves, dwarfs, and giants. Many of the characters of childhood tales well known throughout the world have their origin in the stories grandmothers of the Black Forest region told youngsters many decades ago.

The Black Forest is well known for its cuckoo clocks, its spas, and the colorful folk costumes of the region. It stretches for almost 120 miles, from the city of Karlsruhe to the Swiss border. In the southern part is the highest peak, the Feldberg (4,897 feet). Mountains in the northern part of the Black Forest are not as high and the range is much narrower. Within the region are the tranquil villages and towns to which German city folk like to come in summer. These are resorts with spas where one can rest amid quiet surroundings of great natural beauty. Many spas are famous because of their springs of mineral waters that are said to be beneficial in the treatment of certain diseases. Mud baths, bathing in hot springs, and drinking or inhaling the vapors of mineral waters are a few of the methods used in treatment. Spas are common in many parts of Germany and are well patronized. In some there are casinos where visitors can gamble. They have been popular for many centuries. Ruins of baths built by Romans have been found in some of the well-known spas.

The cuckoo clock was born in the Black Forest. Anton Ketterer is usually credited with having made the first one in 1703. He lived in the village of Schoenwald. While walking home through the forest and thinking about what new toy he could carve for his children, a bird flitted across the path. Why not a clock with a bird that could say

This group is wearing the folk costume of the Black Forest's Gutach Valley.

"cuckoo"? So that evening he set to work. To make the wooden bird "cuckoo" he designed a small bellows patterned after the bellows in the organ of the village church. Like most of the first cuckoo clocks, the one produced by Ketterer was carved entirely from wood, gears and wheels included.

For years, cuckoo clocks were made by craftsmen in their homes in the Black Forest. This practice continues today to a minor degree, but the bulk of production comes from the factories located in several of the towns of the region. One factory in Triberg produces thousands of cuckoo clocks a year.

Visitors to the Black Forest find it a storybook land. Winding roads cling to the hillsides, offering excellent views across narrow green valleys where farmhouses have high-pitched thatch roofs. These Schwarzwald houses have been rapidly decreasing in number in the past few decades. Since thatched roofs are a fire hazard and insurance rates are high, farmers began replacing the thatch with roofs of slate shingles. It soon became clear that none of these picturesque houses would be left in a few years, so laws were enacted which prohibited the removal of the thatched roof of any of the remaining Schwarzwald houses or its repair with any material other than thatch. Some of the finest examples can be found in the Gutach valley. Each provides shelter for farm animals on the ground floor. The farmer and his family live on the second floor where windows open to a balcony spanning the front of the house. The space directly under the roof is for the storage of the winter supply of hay.

Freiburg, one of the largest cities in the Black Forest, is not far from the Rhine and the border of France. Its cathedral, on which construction began in the year 1200, is considered one of the finest in Germany. The steeple, a masterpiece of open rock lacework, rises high above the city. One of the bells in the steeple, cast several hundred years ago, weighs five tons and is called "Hosanna." The University of Freiburg, in the heart of the city, was founded around the middle of the fifteenth century, and today it is one of Germany's leading institutions of higher learning.

Karlsruhe, a city north of the famous spa, Baden-Baden, was planned by Margrave Karl Wilhelm a little more than 250 years ago. The buildings he commissioned to be built amid its parks and wide avenues were in the neoclassical style of architecture. Many were in ruins at the end of World War II but some have been reconstructed. Since the war a number of industries have located in Karlsruhe, because the city has harbor facilities developed to make use of the Rhine. The highest judicial body in Germany, corresponding to our Supreme Court, is located in Karlsruhe. Today the city has a population of over two hundred fifty thousand.

In the tenth century there was a stud farm (*Stutgarten*) in the valley of the Neckar where one of the counts of Wuerttemberg decided to build a castle. Later a town sprang up below the castle, and as it became larger it spread over the site of the farm. Eventually the counts became dukes, and in 1806 the duchy became the kingdom of

Wuerttemberg. The town became the seat of government in the kingdom and was named Stuttgart. A horse appears on its coat of arms.
Today it is the capital of the *Land* and has spread over the surrounding
hills. Many industries are located in Stuttgart including the manufacturing of electrical equipment, cameras, optical instruments, textiles,
and clothing. It is also one of Germany's major publishing centers with
a book fair each winter. But Stuttgart has never completely lost its
rural characteristics and acres of the vineyards that once covered the
hillsides remain within the city.

In 1386 Elector Ruprecht I of the Palatinate established a university in Heidelberg, which soon won recognition as a research and cultural center. The traditions and customs of its students became part of
the life of the city. *The Student Prince,* an operetta based upon the story
of a German prince who came to Heidelberg to study, depicts these
customs. Buildings of the old university, with ancient lecture halls,
stand in the heart of the city beside buildings added in recent years.
The narrow lanes, the tree-lined boulevard along the Neckar River,
the old bridge across the river with towers and portcullis, and the
magnificent castle on the hill help Heidelberg retain its position as one
of Germany's most romantic cities.

Heidelberg suffered no damage in World War II. In the seventeenth
century, however, it was sacked and destroyed by the French army
during the reign of Louis XIV. They blew up the castle. It was par-
tially reconstructed and now, every summer, thousands come to see
the flower show held in its halls and gardens, and the drama festival.
The cellar contains the world's largest wine cask with a capacity of
fifty-six thousand gallons. In early times it was used to receive the wine
brought by the peasants of the Neckar valley in payment of their
taxes.

If you could dine out tonight in a restaurant in Stuttgart or be a
supper guest at the home of one of its farmers, you would enjoy these
local dishes. A welcome item on the menu is ham cooked in brandy. In
many areas onion pie is popular and is usually served with apple

The old Heidelberg Bridge across the Neckar. The portcullis is partly visible through the bridge-gate opening.

cider. Onion pie consists of pie crust heaped with onions cooked in a mixture of butter and cream. Swabian *Spaetzle*, which are oversize noodles, and a large ravioli known as *Maultaschen* are also favorites.

### HESSE

The hilltop castles of margraves, dukes, and counts still contribute to the beauty of the Hessian landscape in the valleys of the Main, the Lahn, and the Fulda. Remnants of medieval villages that snuggled below them have resisted erosion during the centuries. Around them have grown the towns and cities of the modern era. Some villages of timber-framed houses flanking cobblestoned lanes still have walls built in the Middle Ages with watchtowers and turrets reaching toward the sky. There are castles that are crumbling ruins, each the victim of wars that have been fought in the region. Others remain intact with gates open to the hordes of summer tourists that invade their courtyards, roam along their ramparts, and inspect the great halls. Many are museums today, with priceless displays of medieval art, jewels, and armor. Some have become castle-hotels where a weary traveler can trudge up a curving stairway with worn steps of stone, perhaps to the prince's room in the highest tower. Windows in stone walls three or four feet thick offer views across meadows, woodlands, and the gabled roofs of the village below. Each castle has an intriguing history. Each has witnessed romantic events, the pomp of colorful ceremonies, the excitement of tournaments, and great feasts held to honor royal guests. Around some have been woven the fairy tales of storybooks cherished by children today. Schloss Sababurg, deep in the forest of Rheinhardswald north of Kassel, is where Sleeping Beauty is said to have slumbered. Today it is a castle-hotel.

The Odenwald is in that part of southern Hesse which tapers toward the Neckar River along its border with Baden-Wuerttemberg. This mountain range got its name from Odin, the father of Teutonic pagan gods. In this beautiful hill country the valleys are scented by the blossoms of orchard trees earlier than in any other part of the land. The ravines and shady nooks of the Odenwald, according to storybooks, are the homes of dwarfs and goblins. A road in the Odenwald leads to the well mentioned in the Nibelungen saga, where Hagen killed Siegfried. This is also vineyard country where wine grapes are grown on the rock-walled terraces of sunny slopes. The armies of Roman emperors, of Napoleon, and of other leaders ambitious to conquer central Europe, have marched through the Odenwald.

The people of Hesse revere the memory of the Grimm brothers. Their birthplace is a town near Hanau, where the Kinzig River flows into the Main not far from Frankfurt. A monument to them stands in the marketplace. A network of hiking trails has been maintained in the northeastern part of Hesse near medieval Bad Sooden-Allendorf. It is close to the mountain called Hoher Meissner in the Kurhessen Range. According to legend, this is the mountain from whose summit Mother Holle shakes the feathers out of featherbeds. When the first snowflakes begin to fall in winter, German children are told "It's snowing, Frau Holle is emptying her featherbeds." Both Jacob and Wilhelm Grimm collected stories of this kind. Both attended the University of Marburg and were later librarians and professors at universities. They not only explored and interviewed in Hesse, but also searched among ancient manuscripts for stories and clues. In the Rheinhardswald they learned about Red Riding Hood. Dotting the basins and valleys of Hesse are clusters of homes and barns of farmers who till strips of land too small to provide space for crops and farm buildings. The farmer, his wife and sons, and any help he has hired come early in the morning to till the soil, plant, or harvest their crop of potatoes, hay, grain, or vegetables, and return to their homes in the village at sundown. A typical Hessian farmhouse includes at least two separate buildings at right angles to each other facing a small yard. Some are built of brick and consist of two stories; others are half-timbered. The front is flush with the village street. Front windows open from a downstairs living room and upstairs bedrooms. On sunny days featherbeds hang over the window ledges for airing. The living room is used only on special occasions and when guests are entertained. A gate in a high board fence leads from the street to the yard. The entrance to the house is usually a side door. Also facing the yard is the barn with stalls for horses and cattle, haylofts, and pens for pigs and geese.

Life in Hessian farming country is as routine as planting and harvesting. The whole family rises early on summer days. Breakfast is bread and coffee at six or seven. Then horses or oxen are hitched to farm wagons to take workers and tools to the fields. When the work schedule is heavy, housewives join the men in the harvest. Later they return home for a more substantial breakfast, then back to the fields until noontime dinner, the big meal of the day. The menu is likely to include short ribs with sauerkraut, or roasted salt pork. Supper comes when they return from their work in the fields. Long before midnight the farmhouse gates are locked and front shutters closed, and the villagers slumber.

The ancient historic structures of the Romans in Hesse, and reconstructions of those that have become ruins, are extremely interesting. An excellent example is the Roman military camp near Bad Homburg. Remnants of the original wall, the Limes, built across part of Hesse and adjoining lands can be seen here. The wooden palisade was built during the time of the Roman emperor Hadrian in the second century. In the third century a camp of wood and stone construction was erected. It was replaced by one of stone masonry with several buildings. A stone wall was also constructed inside the wooden palisade; a ditch or moat was dug outside the wall, and towers were placed at regular intervals. A century or two later, after Germanic tribesmen had swarmed across the frontier of the empire, the camp and wall were abandoned. In the Middle Ages much of the stonework was removed by peasants. Then late in the nineteenth century considerable interest was taken in this remnant of Roman occupation. Today its reconstruction has been completed. Extensive research in ancient manuscripts and books was undertaken before the project was started, to insure that every detail would be correctly reproduced.

Some less extensive structures are as interesting as the huge fortresses and sprawling monasteries that attract greater attention. The monastery of Lorsch is a building of this kind. In the throne room of this historic shrine Charlemagne often dealt out justice to his subjects. Its walls and ceiling are decorated with delicately colored paintings of angels with musical instruments known to the Franks and Romans but nonexistent today. Guides point to the diagonal grooves in the surface of the stone columns at the entrance to the building. These marks were made by Crusaders, who whetted their swords on the stone, as they left the monastery to continue their journey to the Holy Land.

The largest city in the *Land* is Frankfurt, sprawling across both banks of the Main River and inhabited by nearly seven hundred thousand people. Banking, communications, and industry are important fields of activity. The headquarters of some of Germany's largest banks are located in its financial district. Trains that are almost constantly loading or unloading passengers in the big terminal in the heart of the city link it with all the capitals and industrial centers of Europe. On the outskirts is the Rhine-Main airport, one of the largest in Europe.

The Mercury fountain in Frankfurt looks toward Festival Hall and the trade fair headquarters.

Frankfurt has been an important trade center in Europe since the time of Charlemagne. Its location at the crossing of major trade routes, where the Main River was shallow enough to be forded, contributed to its growth. Traders' caravans brought fabrics, spices, jewelry, glass, and other commodities which were eagerly sought, from the lands bordering the Mediterranean Sea. Furs, amber, and minerals were brought from the north. As the volume of trade increased, Frankfurt's trade fairs attracted merchants from all parts of western Europe. Interest grew with the passing of centuries. In autumn and again in the spring around Easter the trade fairs attract thousands to Frankfurt.

There is much of interest in Frankfurt, although the city is an industrial and trade center and not as attractive as most of the large cities of West Germany. Several of the historical buildings of medieval Frankfurt that were completely destroyed during the last war have been reconstructed. Goethe's house, the *Leinwandhaus* (cloth hall) where goods were displayed during the fairs, the ancient *Rathaus* (city hall), and the Roemerberg or city square have been rebuilt. The Frankfurt zoo is one of the finest in Europe.

There are several large towns in the vicinity of Frankfurt: Hoechst has huge chemical plants, and the leather industry is centered in Offenbach. Automobiles roll off the assembly line in Ruesselsheim. Paper is produced in Darmstadt and near this city are the wells from which natural gas is piped to the big chemical plants at Ludwigshafen.

Wiesbaden, the capital of Hesse, lies a few miles west of Frankfurt. It is a beautiful city with many tree-shaded streets, parks, and fountains. At the Wiesbaden Kurhaus, concerts, recitals, lectures, and dances are held, and there is a large casino. A broad avenue in the heart of the city, the Wilhelmstrasse, is flanked on one side by hotels and shops and on the opposite side by the Kurpark with giant shade trees, a large pond with a fountain, and flower beds. Wiesbaden is Germany's largest spa with a population of nearly two hundred sixty thousand, and was a favorite holiday spot of Kaiser Wilhelm II.

RHINELAND-PALATINATE AND SAARLAND

Two neighboring laender, Rhineland-Palatinate and Saarland, are very different in character. In the former the vineyards and quaint vintners' villages are vitally important to the economy. More than three-fourths of all the wine produced in Germany comes from the grapes grown on the slopes of the hills flanking the Rhine and the Mosel rivers. Saarland produces some wine, but much more important to the economy are the coal deposits and the blast furnaces that extract iron from its ores.

The history and the life of the people of Rhineland-Palatinate center about the Rhine. This great river has been a major artery of commerce ever since the Romans came into the region many centuries ago. Before Roman settlements were made, the Rhine was a natural barrier to tribes migrating southward from the northern wilderness. It flows into the *Land* at the point where it ceases to be the international border with France, just a few miles west of Karlsruhe. The Rhine Gorge, the most beautiful stretch of the river, lies between Bingen and Coblenz.

In the Middle Ages the river was an important source of income for feudal lords who had castles along its path. By the use of barriers, such as chains, across the river they were able to halt traffic and collect toll before it could proceed. Historians claim that between Mainz and Cologne there were at least thirty points where toll was collected. The castles, overlooking the river, were built to defend and enforce their right to collect toll. Attacks by neighbor toll collectors were frequent. Two powerful princes of the church competed for this privilege—the archbishop of Mainz and the archbishop of Trier. Today a journey up the river is a fascinating one. At each bend more castles or castle ruins come into view on distant hilltops.

Trier, Germany's oldest city, is in Rhineland-Palatinate. When Roman emperors made it their residence it served as the northern capital of the empire and was called "the Rome beyond the Alps." Officially the city was founded by Emperor Augustus in 15 B.C.; unofficially, it was a settlement many centuries before the Romans appeared in western Europe. Legend has it that Trier is thirteen hundred years older than Rome itself!

Many remnants of the old Roman city are within the boundaries of the modern manufacturing and wine-marketing Trier of today. Most outstanding is the massive Black Gate—the Porta Nigra. The huge four-story structure is in a remarkable state of preservation. Rock used in its construction has been blackened by centuries. Under its stone arches have passed the helmeted soldiers of Rome, barbarians from the great wilderness clad in the skins of animals, knights of the Middle Ages in armor, Crusaders, monks, and bishops. There is also the amphitheater where captured Teutonic tribesmen were forced to battle wild beasts for the entertainment of the populace. It seated thirty thousand people. One of the Apostles, St. Matthias, is buried in Trier. Considered the city's greatest treasures are the robe of Christ and a nail from the Cross on which He was crucified.

The Mosel River skirts the city of Trier, then flows along a route flanked by cliffs terraced for vineyards until it reaches the Rhine at Coblenz. From these vineyards come some of Germany's finest wines. The Mosel was slowly drying up and becoming too shallow for commercial navigation, but in recent years it was canalized following an agreement between France and Germany. France agreed that the Saarland, which had an independent government economically influenced by France since World War II, should be reunited with Germany if Germany would agree to make the Mosel navigable again. It was reunited with Germany in 1959.

Kaiserslautern, Speyer, and Worms are fairly large cities in this *Land*. Kaiserslautern, a key city on commercial routes to the Saarland and France, is a leading textile-manufacturing center, and the supply center for the North Atlantic Treaty Organization. Speyer has the largest cathedral in Germany; the remains of eight German emperors rest in its vaults. The massive structure was built near the Rhine nine centuries ago. Construction was begun in 1030 by Emperor Conrad II and was completed in 1061, twenty-two years after Conrad's death. It was burned by the French in 1689, during the reign of Louis XIV, and the vaults were opened and plundered. Years later it was rebuilt. New vaults were constructed beneath the choir to form a row of tombs often called "the Choir of Kings." In these tombs lie the remains of Conrad II, Henry III, Henry IV, and Henry V, Philip of Swabia, Rudolph I of Habsburg, Adolph of Nassau, and Albert I. Ironically, Albert I, the son of Rudolph I, lies next to Adolph of Nassau, the man he slew in battle to regain the imperial crown for the house of Habsburg.

Farther down the Rhine is Mainz, capital of Rhineland-Palatinate. In the Middle Ages it was the seat of the powerful archbishops who, as electors, helped choose the emperors of the Holy Roman Empire. Johann Gutenberg, the first European to print books by using movable type, was born here. In his shop, the first Bible printed by this method was produced in 1455. The Gutenberg Museum in Mainz has a workshop reproducing in every detail the one in which this famous printer worked.

At the end of the Rheingau, the stretch below Mainz where the Rhine flows through a wide valley studded with castles and checkered with vineyards, is Bingen. Storybooks have brought fame to Bingen. They tell of the legend of the Mouse Tower built on an island in the Rhine just below the city. This tower, still standing, once belonged to Hatto, archbishop of Mainz, and was used to collect toll from ships on the river. During a famine the archbishop purchased all of the corn that remained from the crop of the previous year. Soon his people had no food and were faced with starvation. They could not pay the price the archbishop asked for his corn. During a feast in the castle the archbishop was approached by a delegation of his starving subjects pleading for corn. Under pretext of granting their request, he led them into one of his barns and then immediately ordered the doors locked and the barn set afire. An army of mice descended upon the castle to punish the archbishop for his cruel deed. He fled to the tower on the island. But mice by the thousand swam to the island, gnawed their way into the tower, and devoured the archbishop.

The Rhine Gorge begins near Bingen and ends near St. Goar. On the bank opposite St. Goar is the promontory famous in Rhine mythology. Here the river is narrow and deep and the current swift, and treacherous rocks lie in its path. The river swerves to gain access to the wide valley just beyond. This is the Lorelei. A tale is told about a maiden with hair that glistened like gold who sat on a rock above the seething waters. When ships entered the dangerous passage, she sang and combed her golden tresses. Her singing distracted the men guiding the ships along the perilous course and, according to the legend, it was she who caused the many shipwrecks at that point on the river.

Saarland is a small *Land* only 991 square miles in area. Most of the 1,132,800 people living within its borders are German. A large part of the labor force works in the coal fields north of Saarbruecken, the land capital and largest city. Coal appears as outcroppings in part of the field, but more is found in a huge deposit deep under layers of sandstone forming what is called the Warndt field. When France signed the Luxembourg Agreement in June, 1956, for the return of the Saar region to Germany, she was given the right to mine coal in the Warndt field for a period of years. Saarland has been using a low-grade iron ore from the Lorraine region in France as a source of iron for making steel. In recent years, however, a high-grade ore from other sources has been obtained for this purpose. Saarland's prosperity fluctuates with the market for coal and steel.

### NORTH RHINE-WESTPHALIA

There are no greater contrasts in all of Germany than in the *Land* of North Rhine-Westphalia. The nation's most modern industrial plants and factories have been built within its borders. Just a few miles from the big cities are farmsteads with quaint half-timbered houses. Ultramodern high-rise apartment houses reach toward the sky in densely populated urban centers. Skilled workmen of the cities where industry is concentrated use the most modern scientific techniques to make steel, plastics, oil, and chemicals. There are still many farmers tilling the red earth who use methods based on the brawn and persistence of sturdy oxen. Villagers cling to folk costumes of past generations, while the feminine population of Duesseldorf eyes the latest creations of fashion experts in the smart shops along the city's busy, chestnut-shaded Koenigsallee. Beneath the surface of the Ruhr district lies enough coal to supply all of Europe for another few hundred years at the present rate of consumption. Meadows, heath, marshlands, and forests lie in its northern and eastern areas where the soil shows no prospect of yielding mineral wealth.

Near the southern border is Bonn, the provisional capital of the German Federal Republic. Bonn was a sleepy little university town until it was selected as the place where the nerve center of government would be until Berlin was free and ready to function as the capital of a united Germany. Government buildings and foreign embassies took form and its population grew to nearly one hundred forty thousand. It is also the birthplace of Beethoven. In the heart of the mining district west of the Rhine is ancient Aachen where the coronations of many of the German emperors of the Holy Roman Empire were held with all the fanfare, pomp, and ceremony customary to such events. Charlemagne drew the attention of the Western World to Aachen by often making it his residence. Aachen, also known by the French name of Aix-la-Chapelle, was once the capital of the Holy Roman Empire.

Farther up the Rhine is Cologne. Its great cathedral can be seen many miles from the city. This famous structure was begun in the thirteenth century and completed six hundred years later. It stands in the heart of the city with traffic swirling about it. Architects point to it as one of the finest examples of Gothic architecture.

Cologne, today, is Germany's third largest city with a population of more than eight hundred fifty thousand, and a center of the trade and industrial area of the lower Rhine valley. Cologne's carnival is one of the gayest and most colorful of any in Germany.

On the maps North Rhine-Westphalia is an irregularly shaped area sprawling both east and west of the Rhine and spilling over into central Germany. Its heart is that densely populated, highly industrialized region known as the Ruhr. Few other parts of continental Europe have a greater concentration of industry. Smokestacks of sprawling manufacturing plants, the fractionating towers of oil refineries, and the bulky forms of blast furnaces break the horizon on the fringes of its large cities. The enormous coal deposits underlying the region furnish fuel and coke for both the Ruhr and the industrial centers of other countries of Europe.

The larger Ruhr cities include Essen, Bochum, Wuppertal, Duisburg, Dortmund, and Gelsenkirchen. Essen is the home of the Krupp Works, and a large percentage of its people are employed in the steel plants and coal mines. Duisburg, on the Rhine, is the largest river port in Europe.

Dortmund, with a population of about six hundred and fifty thousand, has factories, coal mines, and coke ovens. It boasts the largest sports arena in Europe. Solingen, another Ruhr city, was famous during the Middle Ages for the swords it produced. In modern times, the city has converted to the production of high quality cutlery—razor blades, knives, and scissors.

Duesseldorf, with a population of almost seven hundred thousand people, is the financial center for the industries of the Ruhr. The city is actually located south of the Ruhr district, but it is the home of large banking houses and the head offices of large industrial corporations. It also has steel plants and chemical works and is considered a major German cultural center.

Much of Westphalia was once covered by forests of oak. Hogs raised in the region, even during the time of the Romans, fed upon acorns. They became the source of the Westphalian hams which have been famous for centuries.

There are other foods peculiar to this *Land*. One is a mixture of mashed potatoes and apple sauce whipped together called *Himmel und Erde,* heaven and earth. Its name comes from the fact that apples grow on trees and the potatoes grow in the earth. Another dish consists of beans and bacon served in a thick gravy. Pumpernickel, a dark bread, is also popular.

North Rhine-Westphalia, land of coal pits and steel mills, fields and red brick farmhouses, quiet countryside and noisy industrial centers, has an area slightly greater than thirteen thousand square miles. The concentration of mills, factories, refineries, and power plants makes it the industrial heart of the nation. Workers and technicians swarming to its cities and towns have made it the most heavily populated of all the German laender.

## LOWER SAXONY

Lower Saxony includes regions peopled originally by Frisians and Saxons. About 400 B.C. the Frisians colonized the marshlands along the North Sea shore. The Roman writer, Pliny, describes them as a wretched race living on elevated spots in foggy marshlands, or on low hills built to keep their homes from being flooded. These man-made mounds, called *terpens*, were begun at ebb tide. A circular mud wall held back waves. Inside the circle, stilts supported a crude platform on which huts were constructed. Over the years, rubbish and clay filled the space under the platform. Over the centuries new platforms were built above the old to support new huts. In time a solid mound took form.

From their man-made homesites in coastal communities, Frisians went to sea in oaken vessels manned by fifty or sixty oarsmen. They traded with their neighbors, the Swedes and Slavs, and settled on islands in the Frisian or North Sea. The region now occupied by their descendants, and included in the *Land* of Lower Saxony, extends from the Dutch border to the Jadebusen, the large bay where the port of Wilhelmshaven is located. The region is called East Friesland, or Ostfriesland, to distinguish it from the Friesland of neighboring Holland.

In the central and southern part of the *Land* live the Saxons, a people who have played a prominent part in shaping the Germany of today. Saxons were always devoted to their leaders and their gods. When Charlemagne's armies invaded the broad plains between the Rhine and the Elbe to add Saxony to the Frankish Empire, they met stiff resistance. It took more than thirty years of war and the mass slaughter of thirty thousand pagans at Verden on the Aller River before Charlemagne was successful and the Saxons accepted Christianity.

Lower Saxony, known as *Niedersachsen*, has an area of 18,226 square miles and a population of nearly eight million. Hanover is the capital.

Between the Weser River and the Dutch border is a vast plain. Near the sea it consists of lush marshland meadows where horses and cattle graze. Some of this is polderland reclaimed from salt marshes and tidelands by means of dikes and drainage canals. The winds which sweep across this flat country have been enlisted in the work of reclamation. Their force operates huge windmills that pump the water seeping into the lowlands into drainage canals to be carried away.

Inland from the sea and the lush marsh country lies the belt of less productive soil called the *Geest*. It includes moor country, patches of fertile land where crops such as buckwheat can be grown, sparse forests, and heath. The geest was once tilled by the crude implements of Stone Age man and used as pasture for sheep and pigs by the Frisians. Peat is still cut from underlying bogs.

In the vicinity of Lueneburg and in the Altmark region lie the largest heath lands. This is dry country where the melting glaciers of prehistoric times dumped giant boulders. In very early times, when most of this region was covered with heather and scrub juniper, its soil was tilled. Much of the heather has been replaced by the planting of forests of pine, which began in 1768. Those who farm in the heath country grow buckwheat, rye, and potatoes.

Emden is the largest city in the Ems country of Lower Saxony, near the Dutch border. It lies at the mouth of the Ems River. Centuries ago it was a major port until reclamation projects in the latter part of the Middle Ages shifted the mouth of the stream. The opening of the Dortmund-Ems Canal by Prussia in 1899 and the subsequent development of a new harbor gave the city a new lease on life. It again became a great port, receiving iron ore from Sweden and other foreign lands for the steel mills of the Ruhr, and coal from the Ruhr fields for shipment to other parts of Europe.

The Mittelland Canal divides Lower Saxony. To the north lie East Frisia, Oldenburg, and the Lueneburg Heath where agriculture, fishing, and maritime pursuits are of major importance. To the south are manufacturing centers producing textiles, chemicals, and machines.

In the rural areas are small villages with quaint houses built of *Klinker,* a glazed brick. Customs are handed down from generation to generation, and many spring and autumn festivals find their origin in pagan rites intended to win the favor of the gods and increase fertility. These remnants of the past help us picture the people of the medieval times who lived in this marsh and heath country.

In the Lueneburg Heath and near Oldenburg, piles of huge boulders known as the *Huenengraeber* or "graves of the giants" mark the burial places of a people inhabiting the area before the dawn of history.

### SCHLESWIG-HOLSTEIN

Schleswig-Holstein is one of the smaller laender of West Germany. It was formed by uniting the ancient provinces of Schleswig and Holstein with the free city of Luebeck, mother of the Hanseatic League. Its inhabitants are scattered over more than six thousand square miles and live principally in small villages or on isolated farms. The large cities, besides Luebeck, are Kiel, the capital, and Flensburg.

Waterways have always played an important part in the transportation of goods in this part of Germany, though there are few large rivers. It was at the base of the Jutland Peninsula that canals were first built in northern Germany. The city of Luebeck built canals about five hundred years ago to be used in transporting salt and merchandise to the Elbe River farther south. In the eighteenth century, a canal beginning just north of Kiel linked the Baltic with the Eider River on which traffic could continue to the village of Toenning on the North Sea. This waterway proved very useful at the time of the Napoleonic

Wars. In 1887, construction of the North Sea-Baltic or Kiel Canal was begun and was completed eight years later.

Schleswig, once a province of Denmark, lies north of Kiel and the Eider River; Holstein lies south of this line. Both were annexed by Prussia in 1866.

For centuries, the North Frisians of western Schleswig have been adding to their many square miles of rich farming country by waging war on the sea. Reclamation on a large scale began in the seventeenth century. The ancient dikes which ridge the farmlands represent stages in the battle against tide, wind, and flood.

Luebeck is not now the powerful city that it was in the days of the Hanseatic League. It is slightly smaller than Kiel and has a population of nearly two hundred and fifty thousand. It was founded about 1143. In 1226 it became a free city with complete control over its own affairs.

For years Luebeck had reaped huge harvests of herring and cod off the Danish and Norwegian coasts. It had built a fleet to handle the industry and to carry salt to the fishing grounds to preserve the catch. A close association with Lueneburg to the south gave it ample salt supplies from deposits in the vicinity of that city. To protect this lucrative trade from pirates, Luebeck organized a union of port cities—the Hanseatic League near the middle of the thirteenth century.

The league grew rapidly in size and power. Among its members were the major ports of Germany plus some of foreign lands. Its growth made necessary the creation of several administrative units, each with a capital of its own. Luebeck was capital of the unit which included Hamburg and the major Baltic ports. The power of so large a league made itself felt in the world of commerce. Trade increased and pirate nests on Helgoland were wiped out. Hansa representatives in foreign ports attended to shipping problems of league members.

Visitors in Luebeck today still find the salt warehouses on the waterfront and many old structures of the city's adventurous past. Most famous, historically, is the medieval town gate. Tourists also flock to Travemuende, the well-known spa that lies within the city limits.

None leave the proud old Hansa capital without sampling a confection which is a favorite of Luebeck citizens—*Luebecker Marzipan,* made of almonds and sugar.

There are more than a quarter of a million people living in Kiel near the Baltic entrance to the Kiel Canal. Before World War II this was one of the country's greatest naval bases. Today it is primarily a large fishing port, with a shipyard where vessels for the merchant fleet are built.

Flensburg, on the German-Danish border, is a quaint old city of red brick houses and blue slate roofs. It was once a great shipping center and is now a fishing port. Its fish markets provide housewives with the eels for smoked eels, a popular German delicacy. Not far from the city is Gluecksburg Castle, the home of the dukes of Schleswig, members of the royal families of several European nations.

Schleswig, also at the head of a fiord, is a much smaller city. It is famous for its Gottorp Castle and a cathedral built six hundred years ago. The cathedral's beautiful wooden altar was created by Brueggemann, a famous woodcarver.

There are no ports on Schleswig's west coast. The waters for miles off shore are too shallow for navigation by large ships. Ebb tides leave mud flats which link the mainland with some of the nearby islands. There are dikes for miles along the seafront. Dikes or dams have been built to provide a permanent link between the mainland and the larger islands of the North Frisian group. The Hindenburg Dike, built to link the western shore and the largest, most northerly island, Sylt, permits railroad service between the two. And ferries operate between the mainland and the other islands.

The people of Schleswig-Holstein, like those of other parts of Germany, have many special dishes. Rye from the central geest is commonly used to make the black bread baked in stone ovens. Fish and eels, served smoked, marinated or salted, find a prominent place on the daily menu. In port cities, waterfront restaurants catering to sailors serve a dish made of diced meat, potatoes, onions, and pickles called *Labskaus.* The famous Holstein schnitzel is breaded veal cutlets smothered with a fried egg, anchovies, and sliced cucumbers. In the town of Schleswig, seagull eggs are served in several ways.

## BREMEN AND HAMBURG—CITY-STATES

Bremen and Hamburg are Germany's largest ports. Under the new constitution of 1952 each of these cities, proud of the distinction of having been a "Free and Hanseatic City," was designated an individual *Land*. Both were almost totally reduced to debris by air attacks in World War II. The Herculean task of removing the wreckage of ships and harbor installations, ruined buildings, and homes, and meticulously reconstructing treasured historic structures has progressed rapidly. Each city is built on the banks of a river on lowland fringed ei-

View of Bremen and the Weser River.

ther by dune country or by marshlands. Both have similar histories and each has had to defend itself from sea marauders. Both are prosperous when the volume of trade is high.

*Land* Bremen consists of two parts linked by a corridor along the Weser River. One is the city of Bremen; the other, the port of Bremerhaven about forty miles to the north at the mouth of the river. More than six hundred thousand people live in Bremen while Bremerhaven has a population of around one hundred fifty thousand.

Bremen is an ancient city. Twelve centuries ago there were clusters of huts on the banks of the Weser where the city stands today. They were frequently hidden by fog drifting up from the Weser estuary and the North Sea or rising from neighboring marshes. In the eighth century the settlement became a bishop's seat. Then a cathedral was built, and outside the wall that encircled the town the number of houses and craftsmen's shops increased. In the early part of the fourteenth century a wall was constructed around the entire city. Twice during the Thirty Years' War this wall acted as a bulwark against besieging armies.

The city was governed by a council under the control of the archbishop, and conflicts sometimes occurred between the two. During one of these flare-ups in 1336 the archbishop's soldiers burned the carved wood statue of Roland that stood in the square before the town hall. A much larger Roland, sculpted in stone, replaced it and is still standing. Roland was a legendary hero, said to have been a nephew of Charlemagne. His prowess in battle with the Saracens and his feats of great strength spread his name among the people. He took his huge sword from a giant. Statues of this popular hero and his famous sword were erected in a number of cities in northern Germany. The Bremen Roland is the most famous and has become a symbol of civic liberty.

A visitor in Bremen would undoubtedly go first to the town hall where the affairs of the city have been administered for the past six centuries. It has been altered and added to at various times even as recently as the present century. Careful planning, however, has created an architectural masterpiece in which Gothic and Renaissance styles are skillfully blended. On its upper floor is the elaborately decorated assembly room and hall that is the showplace of Bremen. From its heavy-beamed ceiling hang huge chandeliers, asparkle with crystal, and large models of historic sailing ships. The Golden Chamber and the elaborate winding staircase to the gallery built in 1616 are treasures. The cellar (*Ratskeller*) with its store of wines, some of vintages of three or four centuries ago, extends under the whole town hall and beyond to neighboring buildings. Its various caves hold barrels of wine assorted according to vintage. The Rose cellar, for instance, has a huge barrel containing a Ruedesheimer wine of 1653, while Ruedesheimer 1748, 1766, and 1784 are in the Apostle cellar.

Although Bremen was extensively damaged during the air raids in the last war, the town hall was untouched. Brave men, during heavy air raids, effectively disposed of the incendiary bombs that fell on the building, and it suffered no damage. In front of the west facade of the town hall is the monument by Gerhard Marcks commemorating the well-known characters of one of the fairy tales of the Grimm brothers —the Bremen Town Musicians. According to the story, they never actually reached Bremen!

Bremen Town Musicians monument beside the Bremen town hall.

Bremen's overseas port of Bremerhaven was developed after 1827. That year the burgomaster of Bremen arranged to purchase, from the kingdom of Hanover, a fishing village near the mouth of the river. Today ocean liners discharge passengers in Bremerhaven; cargo vessels from world ports unload bales of cotton and wool, tons of grain and tobacco. But Bremerhaven is still, as it was in the beginning, a fish marketing center—one of the largest on the continent.

Hamburg is situated quite differently from Bremen. Although there are some marshlands in its vicinity, it is in a region which is partly geest. Much of the cargo for ships docking at its wharves reaches the port by river boats, canal barges, or trucks using the autobahn. Before

View of the town hall marketplace in Hamburg.

World War II a large part of Hamburg's trade came from regions now behind the Iron Curtain—parts of Czechoslovakia and East Germany. This trade has been lost. Some of the shipping that came into the ports of both Hamburg and Bremen has also been lost to large ports like Rotterdam in the Netherlands. With the development of river ports along the Rhine and Main, and the building of more canals to link river systems in the interior of Germany, shippers have found it more convenient to ship through Dutch ports nearer the mouth of the Rhine. Passenger liners usually moor at the docks at Cuxhaven, Hamburg's port at the mouth of the Elbe River. Cuxhaven's role in the shipping industry of Hamburg is similar to Bremerhaven's role in Bremen's shipping. Hamburg has also compensated for its loss of trade to the Dutch ports by stimulating shipping that involves bulk cargo— oil, grain, ores, cotton, and the like. Huge refineries have been built here in recent years.

Hamburg began as a village near the mouth of the Alster River where it empties into the Elbe. A dam across the Alster formed the lakes around which the city grew. The Aussenalster, surrounded by parks and fine residences, is the largest. The Binnenalster, which is divided from the Aussenalster by the Lombard Bridge, is flanked by wide, busy streets, hotels, and buildings housing the offices of shipping and banking firms. The Kleine Alster is a third, much smaller lake near Hamburg's nineteenth-century town hall or *Rathaus*.

# 9

---

# Berlin—A City Divided

Berlin became the capital of the German Empire in 1871. It grew in both population and importance into one of the great cities of Europe. In the early years of this century Berliners thrilled to the pomp and ceremony of the court of Kaiser Wilhelm II. The fanfare that attended the official visits of world dignitaries became part of their everyday life. Unter den Linden, the broad avenue flanked by linden trees in the heart of the city, was gay with flags, the resplendent uniforms of soldiers and guards, and the music of military bands.

The capital of the country unified by Bismarck and ruled by the Hohenzollerns had grown from two small villages, Berlin and Coelln, on the Spree River. Historians have learned that they existed at least several centuries ago as minor trade centers—villages of huts to which fishermen brought their day's catch. Berlin was on one bank of the Spree River and Coelln was directly across from it on an island in the river. Both were in the Mark of Brandenburg, a frontier province of the Roman Empire. The unproductive sandy soil of the surrounding countryside discouraged agricultural pursuits. Nor were there abundant natural resources on which industry could thrive. The existence of Berlin and Coelln depended solely on the Spree, Elbe, and Havel rivers, water routes for goods brought from distant regions. By the fifteenth century the towns had grown large enough to merge into Coelln-Berlin; later they were known merely as Berlin. Here too an encircling town wall was built. Protection was needed in the desolate

Brandenburg country. Robber barons made forays into neighboring territory from their castles to pounce upon travelers and invade villages, and Berlin was subject to frequent marauding. After Elector Frederick II made it his permanent residence, the town was fortified and expeditions were sent into the wilderness to exterminate the troublesome barons.

Berlin grew rapidly after Brandenburg became the nucleus of the kingdom of Prussia. Swamplands inhabited by fisherfolk were converted by King Frederick William into Potsdam, a beautiful suburb, with quarters for his regiment of tall grenadiers. His son, Frederick the Great, built magnificent Sans Souci Palace a few years later. By 1740 the city's population had reached nearly one hundred thousand. The

The Brandenburg Gate looking toward East Berlin.

Brandenburg Gate at the entrance to Unter den Linden was completed by 1791.

Early in the nineteenth century during Napoleon's reign Berlin was under French occupation for three years. Later when Bismarck had succeeded in uniting many principalities, dukedoms, and kingdoms, he made Berlin the capital of the German Reich. The population of the city was then eight hundred thousand; by 1900 it had reached two million. Just before World War II over four million people lived in the city, which covered an area of 340 square miles.

In 1933 Berlin entered a period in which it was to witness the grave and shameful events of Adolf Hitler's rise to power. In Berlin during the early stages of the Nazi program, works of modern German literature were burned in one of the city's squares. Hitler also ordered his arsonists to burn the Reichstag Building. The city became the headquarters of the Gestapo. On September 1, 1939, from Berlin, Hitler made the announcement that started World War II. The war was to last more than five years—a period which saw the population of the city dwindle to half of its prewar figure. When Allied bombing began, building after building was shattered and engulfed in flames. Street after street was blasted to rubble—the bombs rained upon Berlin in retaliation for the destruction Germany had wrought in the rest of Europe.

The end came in April, 1945. With the city in ruins, Hitler stubbornly persisted in throwing his troops into battle. From his headquarters in the bunker under the ruins of the chancellery he still sent commands to the front. The Russian army was closing in on the city and it was under bombardment by Russian artillery. As Russian troops swarmed into the streets Hitler took his own life. Even after Soviet forces had put an end to all resistance, destruction of the city continued.

Just before the end of the war, Berlin was divided into sectors. Each was put under the control of one of the Allied victors. At first there were three—Great Britain, the Soviet Union, and the United States. Then France became an occupying power, so the city was divided into four sectors. A body called the Kommandatura, consisting of the commandants of each sector, was created to govern the city. A mayor and a council elected by the people conducted municipal affairs subject to Kommandatura approval.

Not many months passed before serious differences arose between the Soviet commandant and those of the other three powers. The Russians tried to win control through the city council elections in the autumn of 1946. When ballots were counted in all sectors, the vote was overwhelmingly anti-Communist. Then a more serious difference arose over stabilization of the mark, and currency reforms to prevent inflation. The Soviet commandant refused to accept West German marks as the currency of the Russian sector and the Soviet officials walked out of the Allied Control Council. They also refused to attend further meetings of the Kommandatura, and resorted to halting traffic on the corridors used by the Allies which linked Berlin with West Germany. When West German marks were declared the only acceptable legal tender in the sectors of the Western powers, the Soviets adopted more drastic measures. They cut all surface lines of communication with the outside world on June 23, 1948. This was the blockade by which Russian authorities hoped to starve West Berliners into submission.

The Allies' response was an airlift. Food, fuel, and other necessities were brought into West Berlin despite frequent harassment by Soviet planes along air corridors. During the eleven months of the Berlin Blockade there were two hundred thousand flights in what became known officially as the Berlin Airlift, and unofficially, among the men who piloted the planes, as "Operation Vittles." During that period about two million tons of supplies were brought in. The Soviet Union eventually saw the futility of their plan. In May, 1949, a Soviet representative met with those of the other three powers in New York and an agreement was reached to end the blockade.

Preparations were made in the spring of 1949 for establishing the Federal German Republic. The sectors of Berlin under control of the Western powers were included with certain restrictions. They became

a *Land* in the Federal German Republic, but their members in the federal legislative body were to have no vote. At the same time the Soviets
fused East Berlin with the German Democratic Republic and made it
the capital of East Germany.

June 17, 1953, was a dark day for East Berlin. Construction workers
objecting to an increase in work quotas by the Council of Ministers,
the governing body of the German Democratic Republic, began a de-
monstration that spread throughout the East Zone. Ulbricht, head of
the East German state, obtained the support of the Soviet occupation
forces. Russian troops and tanks moved against the unarmed demon-
strators to put an end to the uprising.

During the 1950s the Soviets tried to force the Western powers out
of Berlin by threats and ultimatums. Then on Sunday, August 13,
1961, the German Democratic Republic ordered a wall to be constructed around West Berlin. Under the protection of troops and
tanks, a wall of concrete blocks, barbed wire, and control towers was
built, completely dividing the city. The prime motive was not just to
inconvenience West Berliners or force the Western Allies from the city.
West Berlin had become a convenient escape route by which residents
of both East Germany and the occupied lands under Polish administration could reach freedom. A critical shortage of labor, both skilled
and unskilled, plagued the East Zone. Over the years more than three
million had fled through Berlin as refugees to West Germany. To prevent any further lag in reconstruction and production it became necessary to halt this leak of manpower and brainpower to the West.

Attempts are still made to escape from East Berlin. Some have succeeded; others have not—many escapees have lost their lives or been
severely wounded in making the attempt. There has been a smaller
movement eastward by dissatisfied West Germans.

West Berliners are still confident that Berlin will some day be reunited and again be the capital of a united Germany. Today they are
making their part of the city an example of the progress that can be
made in a free democratic society.

Visitors to West Berlin arriving by plane at Tempelhof Airport, one

Building the Berlin wall.

of the largest and busiest in Europe, have a splendid panoramic view. They see the pine forests around the airport, the chain of lakes on either side, the silvery threads of the Spree and Havel rivers, and block after block of brightly painted high-rise apartment houses. In front of the terminals in the *Platz der Luftbruecke* (Place of the Air Bridge) stands the Airlift Monument erected in memory of American and British airmen who died in the 1949 airlift.

In an area which little more than twenty-five years ago was a desert of rubble, there are handsome new buildings. A huge convention hall of ultramodern design has been built to encourage conventions. The old Reichstag Building is being reconstructed to appear as it did in pre-Nazi days. Kurfuerstendamm, formerly a residential street, has become the main shopping street, since the heart of prewar Berlin is now in East Berlin. It is flanked by elegant shops, plush restaurants, and sidewalk cafes. At night it is brilliant with the lights of theaters and night clubs. The Free University was founded in 1948. By the latest count there are well over four hundred bookshops in West Berlin. The Brandenburg Gate on the sector boundary is now repaired and redecorated.

There is plenty to see and do in this island inside Communist territory. It is a crowded metropolis with a population of over two million. Tauenzienstrasse is another bustling street of the new business district built in a residential area of prewar Berlin. Each day at noon the deep tones of the Freedom Bell, which hangs in the belfry of the new town hall in the Schoeneberg district, roll out across the city. This is a replica of the Liberty Bell in Independence Hall in Philadelphia. Many

Ernst Reuter Plaza looking up Strasse des 17 Juni (Street of the Seventeenth of June) in West Berlin today.

events are held at the fairgrounds where, every autumn, the German Industry Fair is scheduled. The Agricultural Exhibition is another annual attraction. Charlottenburg Palace, once the residence of Prussian kings, is an art museum—one of many museums in the city. For relaxation, one can take a boat ride on the canals of the Havel River or bathe at the beach at Wannsee.

Industry has been developed in West Berlin, but because raw materials must be brought in from West Germany production has never equaled the cost of materials. Electrical and electronic manufacturing, publishing, leather and textiles, clothing, food products, and precision tools are among the leading industries in the city.

In contrast to West Berlin, East Berlin has progressed slowly. Some buildings of historical interest have been reconstructed. Along Unter den Linden, which is regaining some of its former elegance, many new buildings have risen. Most of these resemble, in architectural style, buildings common in Moscow. Unter den Linden leads to Marx Engels Platz and Karl Marx Allee. The huge Soviet Embassy Building is in this area, as is the reconstructed St. Marienkirche, the oldest church in the central area of prewar Berlin. Each May Day, East Germany celebrates with a great military procession down Unter den Linden— a reminder of those days when this great avenue was the setting for brilliant colorful processions during the reign of Kaiser Wilhelm II.

# 10

---

# The German Democratic Republic

German people living behind the Iron Curtain faced much greater problems during the period of recovery from World War II than did the people of West Germany. Their progress in reconstruction has been slow, but considering the conditions, the result has been a remarkable achievement.

Their country, which has less than half the area of West Germany, has very limited natural resources. Coal deposits consist of brown coal or lignite, not the hard coking coal required for extracting iron from its ores at low cost. Deposits of iron ore are also scarce. In agriculture the variety of crops that can be grown is relatively small because of the poor soil. Potatoes, corn for fodder, wheat, sugar beets, and barley are the principal farm crops today. Only in recent years have enough tractors been available to work the soil. Livestock killed during the war had to be replaced and good pasture land is not overly abundant. Much of the area now known as East Germany was Prussian, and the Prussians had held the land in large estates which have since been divided into workable areas.

When the Soviets took control of the territory they were eager to exact reparations from the German people to pay for the damage done to Russia, Poland, and other invaded countries. They took over most of the heavy equipment. Industrial plants that had not been destroyed during hostilities were dismantled and shipped to Russia. All of this made reconstruction more difficult. While West Germans were rebuilding with Marshall Plan aid, East Germans, who were trying to do likewise, were also required to support a political revolution in their own land.

Communist authorities worked out five-year plans for East Germany's recovery. In the early fifties heavy industry received top priority. As far as possible, new plants were located in remote, sparsely settled areas. But this was not always satisfactory. For example, after construction was under way on the Stalin iron and steel project, it was discovered there were insufficient deposits of basic materials in the area. Lignite was the only coal available, and making coke from lignite was very costly so the project was halted. Other industrial developments, however, proved extremely successful.

In the late fifties emphasis was placed on the production of industrial chemicals and fertilizers. The manufacture of machines was also given high priority. During this period the *Schwarze Pumpe Kombinat,* a large complex of power stations and coke ovens, was constructed at Cottbus, a city with about sixty thousand inhabitants on the Spree River, near one of the largest fields of brown coal in the country. Processes were soon developed for extracting all the chemicals possible from this coal. The complex was completed and in operation by 1959.

Plans of the East German government were altered as new priorities arose. Emphasis in the early sixties were shifted to electronics, petrochemicals, plastics, and machine tools. A nuclear energy power plant was soon under construction near East Berlin. Not far from Frankfurt, huge blast furnaces for making pig iron were built. The iron ore is obtained from the Soviet Union, and much of the coke from Poland. Steel plants have been built near Dresden and Brandenburg. Tools and metal-working plants are exported to other Communist bloc countries in eastern Europe.

A shortage of petroleum was relieved by construction of the "Friendship" pipeline, which brings oil from the Ural Mountains more than two thousand miles away in the Soviet Union. Cargo vessels, passenger ships, tankers, and ferryboats are built in shipyards along the Baltic coast, many for the export trade. The largest yards are at Rostock and Warnemuende. Petrochemicals are produced in the Schwedt plant. A variety of chemicals from potash, lignite, or limestone are products of plants in Leuna, Schkopau, and Halle. Automobiles come off the assembly lines at Zwickau and Eisenach. Near Karl Marx Stadt, formerly the city of Chemnitz, textiles are made from synthetic fibers.

Scarcity of labor—both skilled and unskilled—has hampered industry. For several years the loss of young people dissatisfied with austerity, domination by the Russians, and the shortage of consumer goods was enormous. They were attracted by the higher pay and greater freedom in the West. Communist methods of control and the use of government informers were resented by many. The Berlin Wall and the precautions along the border between East and West Germany reduced the exodus to a mere trickle. Guards were placed along much of the border, barbed wire barriers were erected, and a wide strip was ploughed to make it easy to track any East Germans who might attempt to escape.

The German Democratic Republic came into existence when a proclamation was made by Soviet authorities on October 7, 1949, and the appointment of William Pieck as president was announced. East Germany, however, was still paying dearly to Russia for her part in World War II. Under the guise of protecting the new republic, the Soviet Union maintains an estimated three hundred thousand troops within the borders of East Germany. This is despite the announcement in the spring of 1954 that the young republic was a sovereign state.

The office of president was abolished in 1960. It was replaced by a council of state and its chairman is the head of state. Since this government post was inaugurated it has been held by Walter Ulbricht who is from Leipzig. Ulbricht left Germany when Hitler came to power and lived in Russia. In Leipzig he had been a cabinetmaker and an ardent Communist party member. The planning, aggressiveness, and persistence of this man has been a prime factor in aligning East Germany with the Soviet Union. Willi Stoph, the present premier—an ap-

"Checkpoint Charlie" entrance to East Berlin through the Berlin Wall.

pointed position—has recently taken a larger role in the government since Ulbricht's failing health has prevented him from carrying out many of his former duties.

East Germany extends from the eastern border of the Federal Republic of Germany to the border of the Polish-administered territory along the Neisse and Oder rivers. From the shores of the Baltic Sea it spreads southward to Czechoslovakia. More than seventeen million people live in this area of 41,659 square miles, slightly larger than the state of Ohio. It includes the former laender of Thuringia, Saxony, Saxony-Anhalt, Brandenburg, and Mecklenburg. The laender were abolished in 1952 and the country divided into fourteen smaller units called *Bezirke*. Each division bears the name of a major city within its borders, which also serves as its capital.

Two large rivers flow through East Germany. The Saale rises in the Fichtelgebirge, a mountain range in West Germany, flows across Thuringia, and joins the Elbe River near the city of Magdeburg. The Elbe River runs northwestward through the cities of Dresden and Wittenberg.

There are forested mountain ranges in the southern portion of East Germany. The Erzgebirge lies along the boundary between it and Czechoslovakia. In the southwest is the Thuringian Forest, and north of this range, the picturesque Harz Mountains. Both are regions where handcrafts have been carried on in peasants' homes for centuries. Woodcarving and the making of musical instruments, glass, and porcelain were developed because forests and mineral deposits supplied the needed materials and agricultural pursuits were not profitable. The Saxon Lowland lies between the Elbe and the Saale, surrounded by mountain ranges. The beautiful alpine scenery along the Elbe River Gorge has furnished inspiration for many an artist and has become known as the "Saxon Switzerland."

Some of the large cities of East Germany are located in this southern part. The largest is Leipzig with a population of about six hundred thousand. The city is a music and book publishing center. The semi-annual Leipzig Fair is a major event in the German Democratic Republic. It has been held since the Middle Ages when medieval trade routes, linking the Mediterranean countries with Hamburg, crossed those leading into the north at Leipzig. Merchants passing through the city were required to unload their goods and offer them for sale at the Fair before moving on.

Dresden, with a population of about five hundred thousand, lies southeast of Leipzig close to the Czechoslovakian border. Its importance as an art center began around 1690, when August the Strong was the Saxon king. In prewar days Dresden china was one of the city's most widely known products. Near the city is the small town of

Meissen which produces fine quality porcelain. The principal products of the region are textiles, paper, metals, and machinery.

In the closing weeks of World War II an air attack was launched against Dresden by the British and Americans. The tens of thousands of bombs that were dropped within a few hours destroyed the city and killed many thousands of people. Some have estimated the death toll to have been well over one hundred thousand. Branded one of the most disgraceful episodes of the war, the attack's military value has been seriously questioned.

The Thuringian region in the southwest part of East Germany consists largely of forest. Its industry is mining and woodcrafts. There are lowlands along the Saale River with farms and small picturesque villages of half-timbered, tile-roofed houses. Porcelain and iron products are made in some of the villages, textiles in others. Jena, one of the larger towns, has long been a center for glass production. Its optical instrument makers turn out fine telescopes, microscopes, and camera lenses. Erfurt, formerly the capital of Thuringia, is now the capital of the Bezirk called Erfurt.

The region of Mecklenburg reaches from the northern limits of Brandenburg to the shores of the Baltic Sea. Its northern part has dry sandy soil. Windmills have been used quite extensively to provide additional water for growing crops. In some areas there are lakes, stretches of heath, and forested hill country. North of the lake district is the part of the Baltic coast commonly known as the Ostsee. Here are the old Hanseatic cities like Rostock and Stralsund. Warnemuende is a favorite seaside beach area. Just off the coast is Ruegen, a beautiful island.

At the end of World War II, the German people living in Silesia, Brandenburg, Pomerania, and East Prussia east of the Oder-Neisse line were driven out. Each inhabitant was permitted to take only a few possessions. About eight million crossed the Oder-Neisse line. A large number found their way into West Germany, adding to the problem of caring for the hungry and homeless in that area. All of the land from which they were driven is now under Polish administration except the extreme northern part of East Prussia, which is now Soviet territory. The future status of these lands remains to be decided when a peace treaty with the four powers is signed.

# 11

---

# Happy Holiday Times

When the first snowfall mantles the countryside, thoughts of Christmas fill the minds of German youngsters. Christmas, the Weihnachtsfest, is their happiest holiday season. There are things to prepare well in advance. When the spicy scent of *Pfefferkuchen* comes from the kitchen in mid-November, that is proof those preparations are under way. Pfefferkuchen, a kind of gingerbread, must be made five or six weeks before Christmas so it will be soft and tempting when the day arrives. After this is made German mothers spend many hours in preparing *Nuernberger Lebkuchen*. From both pfefferkuchen and lebkuchen stars, hearts, and clover leaves are cut and coated with chocolate or sugar icing.

Four Sundays before Christmas the Advent wreath is hung in many homes. A wreath of evergreen twigs supporting four candles hangs from the ceiling by four red ribbons. Each Sunday a candle is lighted until the last Sunday before Christmas when all four burn brightly.

The sixth of December is the red-letter day for German children. Boys and girls set out their shoes for Santa the evening before and awake to find them filled with candies, nuts, and many other good things to eat.

Christmas Eve and Christmas Day are strictly family affairs. The inns, taverns, and restaurants are closed. There is no dancing. All work comes to a standstill on the day before Christmas so that final preparations can be made. In late afternoon, many families attend church; others go to midnight mass. In the evening, after a feast usually of fish, such as carp, presents are distributed. Everyone receives a decorated plate filled with apples, nuts, and pfefferkuchen. Carols are sung while members of the family open their presents and admire the tree. The day after Christmas, dances are held in almost every inn.

On New Year's Eve, or *Sylvester* as it is known in Germany, plenty of punch made from red wine and water seasoned with cloves and sweetened with sugar is served. There are doughnuts filled with marmalade. Just for fun, a few of the doughnuts have fillings of mustard or perhaps a lump of coal. When the hour of midnight draws near, the entire family, each member provided with a spoon and a small lump of lead, gathers around an alcohol lamp. Each in turn holds his spoon above the flame until the lead is melted, then drops the molten metal into cold water. By "reading" the shape of the lead when cooled, an older member of the family tells what the future holds.

Between Christmas and the beginning of Lent, the carnival season gains momentum. Carnival officially begins at eleven o'clock at night on the eleventh day of the eleventh month. It is then that the prince of the Carnival is chosen from candidates who are popular members of the community. His coronation early in the new year marks the beginning of merrymaking. The season's festivities are much like those of the New Orleans Mardi Gras. Revelers, masked and in gay costumes, join in the street dancing and the processions. These festivities reach their peak on Rose Monday and Shrove Tuesday and come to an abrupt end on Ash Wednesday.

The German Easter has its traditions too. A few days before Easter Sunday, youngsters build a nest and hope the Easter rabbit, the *Osterhase*, will fill it with eggs. On Easter Sunday the colored eggs, fastened to a pole by ribbons, are brought to the church to be blessed.

On Thursday night before Easter, fires are extinguished in many homes. Then, at a ceremony in the churchyard on Saturday, a fire is started by the priest. Pieces of wood brought to the churchyard are lighted, and a flame is carried to each house to relight the fires. During this period, from Thursday until Saturday, church bells are silent.

There is an ancient superstition that applies to older people. On Easter morning one must walk alone to the bank of a river or brook, where the water flows toward the rising sun. If one meets nobody along the way and washes one's face in the stream, youth and beauty will be the reward.

The seventh Sunday after Easter, Whitsunday, commemorating the descent of the Holy Spirit, is set aside for religious festivals. On Whitmonday, dances are held in the afternoon.

Thanksgiving Day is an autumn holiday when people go to church to offer thanks for the harvest. The churches are bright with sheaves of grain, horns of plenty, and autumn flowers. In some regions there are processions in which horse-drawn wagons are loaded with different kinds of farm produce and decorated with flowers. Dances are also held on Thanksgiving Day. *Totensonntag*, which is Remembrance Day, comes in November. Graves which have been covered with evergreen twigs to protect the ivy from winter frosts are decorated with wreaths or crosses of evergreens and flowers.

In most towns music festivals are held annually. Those of the larger cities often feature operatic stars from other lands. Small town festivals have choir singing competitions between neighboring villages.

One of the oldest festivals in Germany is Dinkelsbuehl's *Kinderzeche* (children's festival). Records show this celebration has been held since 1635. Some claim it began at a much earlier date. Kinderzeche commemorates an incident during the Thirty Years' War when the Swedish army had completely surrounded the city. The three burgomasters of Dinkelsbuehl were considering a reply to a warning letter received from the Swedish general. They knew full well that cities surrendered to the Swedes were usually destroyed. Dinkelsbuehl, they feared, would be no exception. But lack of food made continued resistance impossible and they finally decided to surrender.

While the burgomasters were deliberating, a shy little girl slipped into the council chamber. She had learned that the Swedish general had just received word of his little son's death. This gave her an idea. However, before she could present her plan the burgomasters left the

Men costumed as the Swedish soldiers who besieged Dinkelsbuehl in the Thirty Years' War.

chamber. But the little girl returned later. She suggested that she and all the children of the city plead with the general. The burgomasters doubted it would succeed, but her plan offered the only chance of saving Dinkelsbuehl from destruction, so they agreed.

When the general was met at the gates, he saw an army of children led by the little girl who was holding the hand of a small yellow-haired boy. The general lifted the little boy up into his arms. Memories of his own son, who had died so suddenly, softened his heart. The pleas of the children moved the general and Dinkelsbuehl was saved.

In the Dinkelsbuehl festival, the children's band, in red and white uniforms, cocked hats, and white wigs, takes over. In parades and pageants of the camp life of the besiegers of Dinkelsbuehl, men wear costumes of the time of the Thirty Years' War. Swedish folk dances are also featured. Visitors come from all over Europe to join in the celebration.

The wine festival held in August in the little town of Cochem in the Mosel Valley is typical of the vintage festivals in most German towns in wine-producing country. The streets of the village are bright with banners. In the marketplace, stands have been erected to support huge wine barrels. After dark there are historical processions with men on foot and on horseback, dressed in costumes of the Middle Ages. Proclamations are read by the town officials. When the band starts playing, there is singing and dancing in the streets. The festival usually runs for three or four days.

Festivals of all kinds are scheduled throughout the year in all parts

Dance around the wine well during a vintage festival in the Mosel valley village of Winningen.

of the land. Many cities and towns have pageants commemorating historical events. Some villages along the rivers and the seacoast have fishermen's festivals. The Munich *Oktoberfest* lasts for the whole month and attracts visitors from all over Germany. These festivals serve to keep alive the ancient customs and traditions of the nation, and to revive interest in folk costumes and music.

# 12

---

# Languages, Legends, and Literature

Teutonic tribes, streaming southward from the shores of the Baltic, brought with them a language that became the mother tongue of Anglo-Saxon, Dutch, Frisian, and modern German. After they settled in coastal lowlands, on offshore islands, and in open areas fringed by forests, language changes took place. The speech of the Franks, Bavarians, and Alemanni living near the margins of the Roman Empire became quite different from that of the Saxons and Frisians out of range of Roman influence. This led eventually to a division of the Germanic peoples into two large language groups. Teutons of the northern lowlands spoke what was called Low German; Teutons in the south, High German. Between these two extremes, a Middle German developed.

Different tribal settlements nurtured local variations. Despite the general use of High German as the standard tongue for Germans, Austrians, and a large part of the Swiss people today, dialects persist in many regions.

A system of writing grew more slowly. Germanic tribesmen knew of the magic symbols scratched on wood or stone by the Norsemen. But they made little use of this knowledge. Not until the second century, when the eastern branch of the flood of migrating Teutons along the lower Danube adopted the alphabet of the Romans, was their influence evident. Latin characters were changed somewhat and made more angular like the Norse or runic symbols.

In the fifth century, when the Roman Catholic church began to dominate western Europe, Latin was considered superior to the German dialects. Legal documents and the literature of the time were written in Latin.

The Middle Ages brought a greater use of German dialects and Gothic script in documents. The first German Bible, printed near the middle of the fifteenth century, was a poor translation. Martin Luther, during his stay in Wartburg Castle, embarked upon a translation of the Bible into a German that could be read and understood in all parts of the land. He used the dialect of the Saxony chancery, modified it considerably, and created a form of High German that became a common language and a strong factor in uniting the German people.

Teutonic tribesmen who settled in the great wilderness of central Europe had no written literature. But tales about gods and heroes spread from tribe to tribe. They chanted and sang these stories before going into battle and when making sacrifices to pagan gods in the sacred groves that were their temples.

These Teutons were at the mercy of the forces of nature. They created gods to interpret these forces. They peopled the forests with dwarfs, elves, sprites, and giants. High among the pagan deities of the Saxons, Franks, and Frisians was Woden, the storm-god who created the winds. Red-bearded Thor, or Donar, hurled shafts of lightning that made the thunder in their wake. Trees, often considered sacred, were worshipped in the flickering light of sacred fires.

The Teutons visualized dwarfs—little men with large heads and long white beards—living underground and doing good or evil. They thought sparkling brooks babbled and gurgled because of water sprites who lived in them. When battles raged, wild Valkyries were believed to swoop into the thick of the fight on white horses and mark the warriors who were to die.

Tales of gods, heroes, and valiant deeds filled the sagas of the Teutons. Greatest of these was the *Nibelungenlied* which was sung for centuries before some unknown poet, using Middle High German, put it in written form. The origin of this national epic is shrouded in mystery. A manuscript of the thirteenth century found in St. Gallen, Switzerland, is said to be its oldest recorded form. There are several versions of the story.

In one version Siegfried, a young prince, leaves his father's palace to win fame. He meets Mimer, an armor maker, who teaches him how to make fine swords. But Mimer soon becomes frightened by the strength of his apprentice and plans to get rid of him. He sends Siegfried into the forest where he unexpectedly meets Fafner, the dragon guarding the treasure of the kings of the Nibelungs, a race of dwarfs. Siegfried draws his sword, slays the dragon and bathes in its blood. The bath leaves his body covered with a horny coating no sword can penetrate except for one spot where a leaf had fallen on his shoulder. From the unguarded hoard, Siegfried takes a ring, a sword, and a magic helmet.

The prince falls in love with Brunhild, queen of Iceland, and goes to see her. He passes through a circle of fire surrounding the island to reach her home. When he departs he gives her the ring of the Nibelungs.

But a spell is cast on Siegfried by Hagen, an enemy, and he helps another man, Gunther, to marry Brunhild. Still under the spell Siegfried marries Gunther's sister Gudrun. Hagen learns from her of Siegfried's vulnerable spot, and he slays the prince as he drinks from a well in the Odenwald.

The tale of Frederick Barbarossa, one of the early emperors of the Holy Roman Empire, is typical of the legends popular with the German people. His death came unexpectedly by drowning while he was leading an army of Crusaders in 1189. The legend claims the beloved emperor is still waiting in a cave in the Kyffhaeuser Mountain in northern Thuringia. When Germany needs him he will return in answer to her call.

The minnesingers were poet-musicians of the Middle Ages who wrote lyrics about love, life in medieval castles, and romance at the courts of feudal lords. Some were nobles and others were merely men attached to noblemen's households. Tyrolean-born Walther von der Vogelweide was the most famous. He accompanied an Austrian duke on a crusade, and upon his return spent several years at Wartburg Castle in Thuringia.

The Meistersingers came into prominence in the latter part of the medieval period. They were organized in guilds which included both singers and the poets who wrote the lyrics. Hans Sachs of Nuremberg, in addition to making boots in Cobblers' Lane, wrote plays. *The Nightingale of Wittenberg* was one of his best. Many years later Richard Wagner made Hans Sachs a character in his opera *The Meistersingers of Nuremberg.*

The introduction of movable type by Johann Gutenberg was also an impetus to literary progress. But the German principalities were devastated by the Thirty Years' War and the advance of literary work was retarded for many decades.

The middle of the eighteenth century saw the beginning of the period of the great masters of German literature. It produced a galaxy of novelists, poets, playwrights, and philosophers. Lessing, Klopstock, Herder, Goethe, Schiller, Kant, and Fichte were among these important men of letters. Johann Wolfgang von Goethe, born in Frankfurt of wealthy parents, studied at both Leipzig and Strassburg universities, and wrote poems, plays, and novels. Among his masterpieces were *Faust, Wilhelm Meister,* and *Goetz von Berlichingen.* Goethe's friend Friedrich von Schiller, whom he met in Weimar in 1784, wrote *William Tell, The Robbers, The Maid of Orleans,* and *The History of the Thirty Years' War.* Schiller had studied medicine and law at Stuttgart and was a surgeon in the Wuerttemberg army before he started to write. This brilliant writer died at the age of forty-six.

Many talented writers contributed to German literature in the nineteenth century. August Wilhelm Schlegel is best known for his German translations of Shakespeare's plays. Heinrich Heine, born of Jewish parents in Duesseldorf, is considered the greatest lyric poet among modern German writers. Because of the persecution to which Jews were subjected, he left his homeland to live in Paris. His *Buch der Lieder* (Book of Songs) was published in 1827. He was the author of *Die Lorelei* which became one of the most widely known of German folk songs. Friedrich Hebbel was an outstanding playwright of the nineteenth century. Two of his plays are still used in German schools—*Die Nibelungen,* based on the epic of medieval times, and *Agnes Bernauer.* A journalist who came from a family of Huguenots, Theodor Fontane, wrote his first novel at the age of sixty and became one of the leading novelists of this period. Many of Fontane's novels were about life in Prussia in the last century.

Jacob and Wilhelm Grimm are known to youngsters all over the world. They traveled from village to village listening to the tales mothers and grandmothers told their children. From the material they gathered they wrote the stories about Little Red Riding Hood, the Frog Prince, Cinderella, Tom Thumb and many other delightful legendary folk that have entertained children for more than a century.

Two outstanding writers of the first half of the present century were Gerhart Hauptmann (1862–1946) and Thomas Mann (1875–1955). Hauptmann, the son of a Silesian innkeeper, wrote many plays and novels. *Die Weber* (The Weavers), was a play about the poverty-stricken weavers of Silesia. *Till Eulenspiegel,* the tale of a country boy from northern Germany; *Atlantis,* a fine novel; and *The Sunken Bell,* his best-known work, helped to bring him the Nobel Prize for Literature in 1912.

Thomas Mann, who was born in Luebeck, championed liberal causes in his writing and because of his political views was forced to leave Germany in 1933 when the Nazis gained control. He came to the United States, became a naturalized citizen, and lived in California for several years. After World War II, he returned to Germany to visit but settled in Switzerland until his death in 1955. *Buddenbrooks* and *The Magic Mountain* are two of his most famous novels. He received the Nobel Literature Prize in 1929.

Ernst Juenger, a prominent twentieth-century author, drew on the adventure and travel he found in his own life as a German army officer in both world wars. His writing attacked the philosophy of Karl Marx and all totalitarian governments. *Der Arbeiter* and *Gaerten und Strassen* are two of his more notable works.

In the fifties, many of the writers who had joined the general exodus of writers in 1933 in protest against Nazi policy returned to Germany. Along with a new generation of writers, they were rapidly gaining world recognition of their works. Hermann Hesse, who had long been considered one of Germany's great novelists, was awarded the Nobel Prize for Literature in 1946. Two of the plays of Rolf Hochhuth, *Soldiers* and *The Delegate*, drew considerable international attention. *Soldiers* was based upon the destruction of Dresden by Allied bombardment. Erich Maria Remarque, who wrote *All Quiet on the Western Front*, was also the author of many works published after World War II, including *Arch of Triumph* and *The Spark of Life*. C. W. Ceram (whose real name is Kurt W. Marek) is known throughout the world for his extremely popular book about archaeology translated into English and entitled *Gods, Graves, and Scholars*. Hans Helmid Kirst, Hans Erich Nossack, and Peter Weiss are also prominent contemporary authors. Peter Weiss, a German Jew, wrote the play *The Investigation*, a drama about the Auschwitz trial which has been presented in theaters of both East and West Germany.

Bertolt Brecht, Guenter Grass, and Heinrich Boell are three of the more recent writers whose works have won them a place among the great contributors to German literature. During the period of the Third Reich Brecht's poems and plays expressed his anti-Nazi views. Brecht was born in Augsburg, but in 1933 he fled from Germany to the Soviet Union, and in 1941 to the United States. After World War II he returned to Europe and went to East Germany. There, in 1949, he formed the theatrical company known as Bertolt Brecht's Berliner Ensemble to produce his plays in East Berlin. *Die Dreigroschenoper*, presented in the United States as *The Threepenny Opera*, is considered one of

Brecht's best plays. Guenter Grass, a novelist of the postwar period, gained international recognition with his *The Tin Drum* and *Dog Years*. Both are satirical novels about the Nazi period. In *Dog Years* Grass wrote of the fate of Hitler's favorite dog, Prince. Heinrich Boell attacked the hypocrisies of the "new Germany" in his writings.

# 13

---

# Music and Art

The early development of German music is linked with either the church or the court of an emperor or nobleman. It was customary for a royal household to require the services of trumpeters and drummers for a variety of ceremonies. Fiddlers were needed to provide music for dances. In some of the monasteries music was taught to promising youngsters. Many a famous composer began his career as a church organist. In the fourteenth and fifteenth centuries most of the masters of music were organists.

One of the most famous musicians of the Middle Ages was the blind organist Konrad Paumann of Nuremberg. He was given a position in the household of the duke of Bavaria in Munich. The city of Munich had many shops where craftsmen produced the finest organs and wind instruments of the period.

Since Venice was the music capital of Europe in the sixteenth century, many talented young Germans went to Italy to study. During this period there was a great demand for Flemish and Italian musicians and singers. Italian choirs and opera singers were brought to Germany to perform in the large cities. The classical period in German music began late in the sixteenth century and produced a number of great composers. Many were helped to start their careers by princes who had a great interest in music and the arts.

Johann Sebastian Bach (1685–1750) was born in Eisenach in Thuringia of a family that had been musicians for generations. Unlike other great composers who struggled desperately for the opportunity to study, Bach grew up surrounded by music. His first position was as a choirboy in Lueneburg. Later the duke of Weimar hired him as a violinist, organist, and orchestra director. Bach finally became cantor of Leipzig's Thomaskirche and taught music in the church school. He spent the remainder of his life in Leipzig. His Brandenburg Concertos, *The Well-Tempered Clavier* and the St. Matthew Passion are just a few of his great compositions.

Wolfgang Amadeus Mozart, perhaps the greatest and certainly the most prolific of the classic composers, was born in Salzburg, Austria. He is often considered a German composer, however, because his family came from Augsburg.

Ludwig van Beethoven (1770–1827) had a more difficult time than Bach. His boyhood was not a happy one. His father, a Bonn musician, quickly recognized the boy's unusual talent. He wanted his son to become a child wonder like Mozart and forced young Ludwig to spend many hours in practice. Beethoven moved to Vienna where he studied under some of the great musicians of the time. Influential friends helped him to gain recognition and there in Vienna he produced the great symphonic masterpieces that still thrill music lovers.

Another great composer, George Frederick Handel (1685–1759) was born in Germany. He was the son of a barber-surgeon at the court. His father frowned on his interest in music, so he had to study and practice secretly until the duke overheard him playing the organ. His father was finally persuaded to permit young George to take music lessons in Halle. Handel's career in music began as an organist in the cathedral of his birthplace. His first opera, *Almira,* was produced in Hamburg when he was twenty. He went to Italy to study and wrote the opera *Agrippina* for performance in Venice. Eventually he traveled to London and became a naturalized Englishman. Handel continued to compose and *The Beggar's Opera* was a great success in the English capital.

Two of Germany's nineteenth-century musical immortals were born in Hamburg. One was Johannes Brahms; the other, Felix von Men-

Beethoven's birthplace in Bonn is maintained to look as it did when the composer lived there.

delssohn-Bartholdi. Brahms was the son of a musician in Hamburg's city theater but spent little time in the city of his birth; most of his life was spent in Vienna. Mendelssohn composed his greatest masterpiece —*A Midsummer Night's Dream*—when he was only seventeen. He was also known for his excellent violin concertos.

Richard Strauss, born in Munich, spent the early part of his life as conductor of the Court Opera there. He also conducted in Weimar, Berlin, and jointly with Franz Schalk at the Vienna State Opera from 1919 to 1924. During the period from 1924 through World War II, his time was largely devoted to composing operas, symphonies, and ballets. *Der Rosenkavalier,* an opera completed in 1911, is one of his best-known compositions.

Since the beginning of the century, a number of German composers have attained international stature. A new trend toward purer abstract music gained favor and men like Paul Hindemith and Carl Orff were among the composers noted for their modern interpretations. Gustav Mahler's symphonic masterpieces have gained wider recognition in recent years. Hanz Pfitzner earned fame with his opera *Palestrina*. *The Threepenny Opera* is the best known of Kurt Weill's musical plays. It was composed in collaboration with Bertolt Brecht as the librettist and produced in 1928. The children's favorite opera *Hansel and Gretel* was created by Engelbert Humperdinck, who used delightful German folksongs as his inspiration for the music. Werner Egk and Wolfgang Fortner are two notable contemporary composers.

Like music, German painting was linked with the church in the beginning. Much of the earliest German painting consists of illuminated manuscripts and books. Along the margins of pages, and embellishing titles and capital letters, were figures, scenes, floral designs, and scrolls hand painted by monks and their students.

Sculptors in other European countries used stone or marble as their media. In Germany, however, some of the finest work was created by sculptors who carved wood. Altars, figurines of saints, pulpits, all manner of church ornamentation were created by such masters of woodcarving as Tilman Riemenschneider (1468–1531). In the Kurpfaelzisches Museum in Heidelberg is one of Riemenschneider's finest creations—the Twelve Apostles Altar. In St. Jakob's Church in Rothenburg another of the magnificent altarpieces he carved can be seen. Throughout Germany, one can find his masterpieces in churches, abbeys, monasteries, and the chapels of castles.

Although Germany has had a smaller number of painters than Holland or France, there are several whose work places them among the masters of art. Albrecht Duerer, who was born in Nuremberg in 1471, was both a painter and an engraver. Perhaps his most widely known work is the *Praying Hands*. What is generally considered his greatest masterpiece is the painting now in the Munich Gallery—*The Four Apostles*. Duerer's *Virgin and Child* and *Madonna and Child with St. Anne* are in the Metropolitan Museum of Art in New York. Mathias Gruenwald, another great artist, lived in the same period as Duerer.

At the close of the nineteenth century modern art in Germany lagged far behind that of France. Germany did not become unified until 1871 and the new nation formed at that time was dominated by ultraconservative, militaristic Prussia. Consequently impressionism, the art movement concerned with painting the effects of light on a subject, ignoring minor details and diffusing the outlines of forms, came late. However, German painters learned of this movement through study with French masters in Paris.

One of the first German impressionists was Max Liebermann, a German Jew living in Berlin. Many of his paintings depicted the life of Dutch peasants and poor working-class Germans. Kaethe Kollwitz also chose subjects for her paintings which dealt with the agony and hardships of the poor. Her work was so distasteful to Kaiser Wilhelm that he cancelled the award of a gold medal that was to be given in recognition of her excellent work.

Expressionism, which emphasizes the painter's emotional experience and is not concerned with realistic representation, developed in Germany in the twentieth century. Emil Nolde, son of a Frisian peasant, was an expressionist who painted religious scenes, landscapes, and figures. Hundreds of his paintings were among those branded "degenerate" art by the Nazis in the 1930s and confiscated.

A group of expressionists called *"Die Bruecke"* was formed in Dresden in 1905. Ernst Ludwig Kirchner was one of its leaders. He produced many outstanding paintings and woodcuts, among them *Street Corner, Gas Tank,* and *Sick Woman.* Kirchner credited the poems of the American Walt Whitman for much of his outlook on life so commonly reflected in his paintings, particularly Whitman's *Leaves of Grass.* In 1917 Kirchner moved to Switzerland. During the Nazi art purge more than six hundred of his works were confiscated. Since he was an extremely sensitive man, it is claimed that this loss had much to do with his suicide the following year. Another of the *Die Bruecke* group whose works were condemned by the Nazis was Karl Schmidt-Rottluff, famous as both a printmaker and painter. One of his finest paintings, *Rain Clouds, Lago di Garda,* was made during a trip to Italy with the famous sculptor Georg Kolbe in 1923. Eric Heckel, a co-founder of *Die Bruecke*, was born near Chemnitz in 1883. His famous *Ostend Madonna* was painted on a piece of tent canvas in 1915.

Other outstanding painters of this period are Franz Marc, August Macke, and Max Beckmann. *Red Horses, Blue Horses, The Yellow Cow*, and *The Tower of Blue Horses* are excellent examples of Marc's work. To use his own words, he "found man ugly; animals, cleaner and more beautiful." This great artist worked furiously during his short life and produced hundreds of paintings, both oil and watercolor. One of his closest friends was August Macke, whose early paintings were impressionistic; those produced in the last few years of his life followed the cubist trend. Like many German artists, Macke studied under the great French painters, Cézanne and Delaunay. Max Beckmann started drawing and painting at an early age and his work spans several modern European movements. He changed from one art trend to another as events affected him. In 1938 he fled to Amsterdam and later migrated to the United States. George Grosz and Max Ernst were abstract surrealists and founders of Dadaism.

In 1919 a school of design was founded in Weimar—*Die Staatliche Bauhaus Weimar*, commonly called Bauhaus. The founder, Walter Gropius, was a brilliant German architect. Ludwig Mies van der Rohe worked with him on the project. Students at Bauhaus studied art forms, crafts, aesthetic values, sociology, and other disciplines in an effort to bridge the gap between art and craftsmanship. The faculty included painters, architects, and sculptors, each brilliant in his field. Among the Bauhaus teachers were Paul Klee, Wassily Kandinsky, and Josef Albers. Also on the staff was Gerhard Marks, the sculptor. Paul Klee was born in Switzerland and studied in Paris. In his abstract art he used many of the methods and symbols that children use in their drawings. A good example of his work is the painting entitled *The Zoo*. Kandinsky, a Russian who had taught at the University of Moscow, had emigrated to Munich. Albers, a German, based his painting on squares of color to free himself of problems which might arise in depicting form. Within a few years of the school's founding, the people of Weimar became quite hostile toward it. In 1925 it was moved to Dessau. A few years later, during the Nazi art purge, it was ordered closed.

The influence of the Bauhaus on modern art continued, however. Its founders, most of the men on the faculty, and many of its students left Germany for the United States. Gropius taught at Harvard. Laszlo Moholy-Nager founded a similar school, the New Bauhaus, in Chicago. It later became known as the Chicago Institute of Design.

Today there are many abstract painters in Germany, but many of the younger generation are turning to more objective forms of art. Included among the outstanding postwar artists are Fritz Winter, George Meistermann, Theodor Werner, and Hans Hoffenrichter.

When Hitler launched his purge of what the Nazis called "degenerate" art, there was a general exodus from Germany of sculptors as well as painters. The Nazis favored sculptures which represented athletic figures. Therefore some sculptors who remained in Germany profited by the great demand for their work. The most outstanding was Georg Kolbe, who had studied under Rodin. His work adorned the structures in the Sports Center in Berlin during the Olympic Games held there in 1936, as did the stone athletes created by another notable sculptor, Arno Breker. New structures designed by today's architects have created a demand for modern sculptures—both expressionistic and realistic. Among the sculptors of the past few years whose work has won recognition are Gerhard Marks, Heinrich Kirchner, Fritz Koenig, and Kurt Lehmann.

# 14

## Science and Industry

The world has applauded German achievements in science and industry. Two world wars left the industrial centers of the country a mass of rubble and its transportation systems a tangle of ruins. In a surprisingly short span of years the wounds have healed and cities have been rebuilt. German products have again entered world markets and many scientific discoveries have been made in German research laboratories.

Germany has always lacked domestic sources of many raw materials essential to a major industrial nation. She has had no extensive colonial empire to supply them. But she has had the advantage of having many scientists, products of her great universities, who learned to synthesize or duplicate the raw materials that were lacking. In their retorts and test tubes men of science built drugs, dyes, plastics, oils, and fibers—a world of new scientific creations. They tackled the problem with a zest that put handcrafts in the background and created industrial areas with sprawling plants and research laboratories along the Ruhr, the Main, and the lower Rhine.

But handcrafts were not permitted to die. They were kept alive in the little villages of Hesse, Baden-Wuerttemberg, Bavaria, and Westphalia. Some of the most treasured products of modern Germany come from the homes or small shops of its craftsmen.

Workshops in Erbach, where ivory carving was introduced in 1783 by Count Franz von Erbach, have produced a stream of delicately carved cameos, fans, crucifixes, and statuettes, bringing fame to this village. The Erbach craftsman takes pride in his work. His skilled hands manipulate the knives, brushes, and tiny drills. With the expertness of an artist, he uses the etching acids, bleaches, and pumice or chalk polishes. Techniques have been passed from father to son or learned in Erbach's school of ivory carving. The ancient castle of Count Franz exhibits the finest examples of the craft in its Ivory Museum.

Refugee German artists from art glass centers in Czechoslovakia moved to Bavaria at the end of World War II. In their new Bavarian shops, they used their skills to create cut glass and ornaments that are still purchased by gift and holiday shoppers throughout Germany. Each family of artisans has its distinctive designs and colors. Woodcarvers and makers of fine musical instruments are also found in many Bavarian villages.

Mathias Klotz was the first to make violins in the Bavarian town of Mittenwald. While he was a child, his parents sent him to Cremona in Italy to learn the art of violin making from Italian master craftsmen. Upon his return he opened a shop in the village. This was in the seventeenth century. The sons of Klotz learned the trade from their father. Violins from Mittenwald became known throughout Europe. More shops were opened in the village. Today Mittenwald is a major producer of fine violins and zithers.

German industry has a fascinating history. It began in the Middle Ages, when craftsmen engaged in producing the leather goods, textiles, metalware, and pottery set up their shops near one another, establishing villages. Artisans engaged in one particular craft usually had shops along a certain lane or street. They were members of a guild which enforced strict regulations regarding apprenticeships, the kind of clothing its members could wear, and other details of their daily life.

Machines using steam as a source of energy were introduced in the nineteenth century. But the sudden industrial changeover began about 1870 with new types of powerful machines and new methods of

Monument to Mathias Klotz, the violin-maker of Mittenwald.

making steel. It marked the beginning of an upsurge in scientific investigation.

German scientists played vital roles in the industrial revolution. Fritz Haber, born in Breslau in 1868, made a discovery of tremendous importance. In his laboratory he found that nitrogen from the air and hydrogen obtained from water could be united to produce nitrogen compounds. He was successful in harnessing a chemical reaction to the needs of industry by using those strange substances called catalysts which either speed up or slow down such chemical changes. He and a fellow scientist, Carl Bosch, worked out the details of what is known as nitrogen fixation. The nitrogen compounds prepared by this method enriched Germany's poor soil and freed her from dependence upon imports of Chilean guano for materials needed in the manufacture of explosives.

Robert Bunsen, a professor at Heidelberg University, did research in the field of electro- and photochemistry. Among Germany's organic chemists was Adolf von Baeyer, the first to make indigo, the blue dye, by synthetic methods. Justus Liebig became known as the father of agricultural and food chemistry. By treating the poor soil of a farm plot with nitrogen compounds, he restored its fertility and it yielded bumper crops. His experiment proved that synthetic chemical fertilizer could be used in place of natural fertilizers. Other chemists who made brilliant discoveries were Emil Fischer in organic chemistry, Wilhelm Ostwald in dye chemistry, and Carl Duisberg, who founded the huge chemical corporation known as I. G. Farben Company.

Men who were geniuses in organizing and expanding industries had a major role in converting an agrarian Germany into an industrial giant. In 1812 Friedrich Krupp produced an excellent quality of cast steel for making cannons in his small forge in Essen on the banks of the Ruhr. After this discovery his plant expanded rapidly to include a number of furnaces. His son Alfred continued his work, produced better steel, and improved ways of making armor plate. But it was the grandson of the original cannon maker, Friedrich Alfred Krupp, a genius in industrial organization, who built the Krupp Iron and Steel Works into one of the greatest industrial corporations the world has ever seen. It was between the two world wars that cartels were formed. These were syndicates of several powerful companies banded together to control the price of their products, the availability of supplies, and world trade. Corporations in other parts of the world linked with German companies in order to establish international trade monopolies. Cartels became so powerful that they have been banned for many years.

A new plan to stabilize prices and employment and meet the needs of all European nations in regard to coal, coke, and steel developed after World War II. This is the Schumann Plan that went into operation in 1953. A common market for coal, iron ore, scrap metal, and steel derived from Germany, France, Italy, Belgium, the Netherlands, and Luxembourg was formed. The companies producing these materials are under private operation, but the flow of their output and distribution of raw materials is determined by a council consisting of representatives from each country called the European Coal and Steel Community. The organization has power to overrule the desires of any individual nation in the pact. Its ultimate purpose is to prevent vital substances from going into armaments production.

German scientists have made important discoveries in fields not directly connected with industry. A story is told about Friedrich Kekule's solution to one of organic chemistry's problems through an idea which came to him in a dream. He had been struggling to learn how hydrogen and carbon atoms link to form molecules of benzene. He dreamed of snakes writhing about, forming rings by biting their own tails. The dream gave him the idea on which to base his theory of ring structure in hydrocarbons. In 1828, Friedrich Woehler synthesized urea and thus disproved the theory that organic compounds could not be produced outside a living plant or animal.

The story of the archaeologist Heinrich Schliemann is like an Arabian Night's tale. He began life as a poor boy in Mecklenburg, the son of a minister. Homer's great epics the *Iliad* and *Odyssey* thrilled young Schliemann. He vowed he would some day prove that these were true stories and not legends. He had amassed a fortune as a successful merchant by the time he reached middle age and decided it was time to carry out his boyhood dreams. On a trip to Asia Minor he unearthed the city of Troy and its archaeological treasures.

Medicine received its contributions from Germany's men of science. Diphtheria was conquered by the discovery of an antitoxin by Emil von Behring. Paul Ehrlich who became director of Germany's Royal Institute for Serum Research in 1896, was one of the winners of the Nobel Prize for Medicine in 1908. He discovered salvarsan and its value in treating syphilis. Robert Koch discovered the cause of tuberculosis and of cholera.

Astronomy and physics profited also. The work of Karl Gauss in magnetism, and of Robert Kirchhoff, who worked with Bunsen at Heidelberg, in spectrum analysis, was important. Carl Friedrich von Weizsaecker made discoveries about the origin of planets. Arthur Korn pioneered in television. Count von Zeppelin built the world's first successful lighter-than-air craft. Messerschmitt, Porsche, Benz, and Daimler developed motors and motor cars. And more recently, Germany has produced a number of rocket and missile experts. Werner von Braun, now director of American missile development in Huntsville, Alabama, and an American citizen, was once Germany's foremost rocket engineer.

# 15

---

# The New Germany

July 1, 1948, marked the beginning of meetings between American, French, and British military governors and presidents of the eleven laender of their occupation zones. A council of representatives from *Land* legislatures met to form a constitution in Bonn with Dr. Konrad Adenauer as its chairman.

The provisional government set up for the control of the new Germany outside the Soviet zone included a president, a chancellor, and a parliament of two houses. The president is elected by a federal assembly consisting of all the members of the *Bundestag* (the lower house) and an equal number of members chosen from the legislatures of the various laender. His term of office is five years. The chancellor, the operating head of the government, is the most important political figure. He is dependent upon the support of one of the parties in the Bundestag or a coalition of parties. Election is by the Bundestag and his term is four years unless he is deprived of his position by action of this body. The Bundestag is elected by popular vote; the upper house, the *Bundesrat,* is appointed by the laender governments. West Berlin has twenty-two nonvoting deputies in the Bundestag's total membership. In 1970 the total number of voting members was 499. Dr. Theodor Heuss was elected president of the Federal Republic in September, 1949, and Dr. Konrad Adenauer, the first chancellor. The Federal Republic has a high court very much like the Supreme Court of the

United States. It includes the *Bundesverfassungsgericht* and the *Bundesgerichtshof* which meet in Karlsruhe.

Political parties were permitted without restraint in all but the Soviet zone by 1950. The major parties in West Germany are the Christian Democratic Union, Social Democrats, Free Democrats, and a small National Democratic party (NDP), a neo-Nazi group.

No peace treaty could be arranged with all of Germany because of Soviet Russia's refusal to enter into such negotiations. But in 1952 agreements were signed by France, Britain, and the United States which made the Federal Republic a sovereign state.

Men who had not supported the Nazis were selected by the commanders of the occupying forces to serve as administrative officials. One was Konrad Adenauer, born in Cologne on January 5, 1876. His accomplishments during his school years were far from spectacular, but he was persistent in working toward the goals he had set for himself. In 1917 he became mayor of Cologne and held the position until Hitler took control of the country in 1933. The Nazis were suspicious of Adenauer. Every effort was made to find some excuse for removing him from office. Finally he was accused of plotting with the French near the end of World War I to make the Rhineland a separate republic. Without warning he was dismissed as mayor of Cologne, arrested by the Gestapo and placed in a concentration camp. Eventually he cleared himself of the charges. To avoid further difficulties he went into hiding. His wife was arrested for refusing to reveal his whereabouts. Fearful for the safety of their children, she eventually gave the Gestapo the information they demanded. Then Adenauer was arrested a second time and released a few months later.

When the American forces arrived in Cologne in the spring of 1945, Adenauer was asked to accept the position of mayor. Cologne was in the British zone, however, and a British general not satisfied with Adenauer's work removed him from his position as mayor.

Adenauer was considered a conservative. He would listen to criticism of his views and proposals, but was determined that his decisions should be followed. He was a devout Catholic and a staunch foe of

Prussian domination. After his dismissal by the British he was chosen leader of the Christian Democratic Union (CDU). When the Western powers permitted the formation of the Federal Republic of Germany in 1949, the CDU worked to have him elected chancellor. By an extremely small margin, Adenauer won. The man from Cologne now had the responsibility of making democratic government a success among a people accustomed to being subjects, not citizens.

Adenauer insisted on maintaining strong ties with the United States as a defense against the threat of the Soviet Union in the east. He also worked hard toward removing traditional grievances that had so long existed between Germany and France, and encouraged continued support of NATO (North Atlantic Treaty Organization). With the help of Ludwig Erhard, Adenauer's minister of economics, West Germany entered an era of great prosperity and became a leading industrial nation. He brought about the release of thousands of German prisoners of war by the Soviet Union and tried to reunite Germany, but without success. For fourteen years, Konrad Adenauer led his country through the critical years of recovery and the establishment of democratic government. He was popular with his people who affectionately dubbed him *"der Alte"* (the old man). He retired reluctantly in 1963 and died in 1967.

While Konrad Adenauer dominated the political scene in West Germany for more than a decade, other political leaders were gaining stature and prominence. As the years passed the chances of permanently establishing a democracy increased. The older generation of Germans, accustomed to following a leader without taking an active part in decision-making themselves, was gradually being replaced by a younger generation with new views about politics.

Ludwig Erhard succeeded Adenauer as chancellor of the Federal Republic of Germany in 1963. Theodor Heuss, the republic's first president, served two five-year terms and was succeeded by Heinrich Luebke in 1959. Erhard was the man largely responsible for bringing West Germany to its feet financially and industrially and into a period of booming prosperity. When a lull came, however, he lost popularity

Cologne's new skyline and promenade along the Rhine has been formed in the years since World War II. Its famous cathedral, which was damaged during the war, can be seen in the background.

and was defeated by Kurt Georg Kiesinger in 1966. Kiesinger's support in the Bundestag was not strong. After serving three years as chancellor, he met defeat by a coalition of Social Democrats and Free Democrats which gave the office to Willy Brandt. Dr. Gustav Heinemann became president in 1969.

Herbert Frahm was born in Luebeck in northern Germany on December 18, 1913. His early life was marked by hardship and poverty. Young Frahm became active in Social Democrat youth groups and was strongly opposed to Hitler and the Nazis. With the rise of the Nazis he was in great danger of being arrested so he fled to Norway. To conceal his identity he changed his name to Willy Brandt when he reached Oslo. In Oslo he became a newspaper correspondent and a Norwegian citizen. Brandt joined the Norwegian army. This reduced the danger of his being discovered. Later Norway was invaded by the Germans and came under Nazi control. For a time Norwegian soldiers were prisoners in their own country. Since this increased the possibility of Brandt's identification he fled to the Swedish border and remained in Sweden until the war was over. In 1945 he returned to his homeland to renew his German citizenship and again become active in the Social Democratic party. But he kept the name of Willy Brandt. He went to West Berlin, became editor of one of the city's leading newspapers, and eventually, in 1957, was elected mayor. One of his goals was to normalize relations between his homeland and the nations under Communist control and the Soviet Union. This has also been a major goal since his election as chancellor of West Germany in 1969.

The new Germany has many characteristics unknown when Hitler was in power or a Hohenzollern kaiser ruled the land. Big cities have new skylines in modern architectural styles. Rebuilding progressed rapidly after the debris of war was cleared away. Cities were carefully planned. Some innovations, such as the transportation system worked out by the city of Hamburg, are being copied in other parts of the world. The increased number of automobiles and the absence of a legal speed limit on the autobahn have led to the highest traffic death rate in proportion to total population of any country in Europe. Supermarkets and shopping centers have sprung up in large cities and towns. There are also motels, although they have not gained the popularity they have in America.

The tastes and the moods of the people, particularly of the younger generation, have undergone great change. Appreciation of art, opera, and fine music is still a German characteristic. But rock-and-roll music has invaded the land and been welcomed by German youth. Lederhosen have lost their popularity to jeans among the young and folk costumes are worn only in small or remote villages during festivals or holiday gatherings. A growing concern for the preservation of historical buildings and sites has led to meticulous reconstruction of many that were damaged or destroyed. There has been an increase in the number of places set aside as national parks and monuments and antipollution activity is taking hold.

Prosperity is widespread; production of steel, oil, and other commodities has gone far beyond previous peaks in prewar days. A serious labor shortage has brought thousands of workers from Italy, Spain, and Greece.

The trade union movement in West Germany has made great progress. German unions are conservative and do not take part in politics to the extent of urging their members to support any certain political party. They are strongly anti-Communist. There have been very few strikes. Union and management representatives have worked together in settling grievances peacefully with only one or two exceptions. This policy has led to greater productivity and has strengthened the industrial growth of the nation. The trade union federation, the DGB, has

Cologne's new bridge across the Rhine has become a symbol of German reconstruction.

maintained modern well-equipped schools for its members and has worked toward insuring its members a role in determining the policy of various industries as to growth and marketing of products. Its overall aim is to better working conditions, increase job security, and contribute to the working man's skills and cultural development.

For several years after the war West Germany was not permitted a defense force of its own. In 1954 the Federal Republic was admitted to NATO and allowed to form a purely defensive armed force—the *Bundeswehr*. This was primarily to give some added security against the threat of invasion by a large Red army maintained in East Germany. The Bundeswehr has close to half a million men in its various branches, most of them in the army. The air force and the navy are relatively small.

Prior to the Hitler years, there were at least five hundred thousand German Jews. A general exodus began in the thirties to avoid Nazi persecution. The departure of Jewish professors from the universities, doctors from medical centers, and writers, artists, and scientists left a vacuum in German scientific and cultural centers that as yet has not been filled. The Nazi crime of putting to death millions of Jews, many from Poland, Czechoslovakia, the Netherlands, Austria, and other Nazi-occupied territories, is one that cannot easily be forgotten. Some Jews have returned to the Federal Republic to again enter professions in law, medicine, and several scientific fields. The estimate of the number of returnees is about thirty to thirty-five thousand. In East Germany, where the Communists are in control, only about fifteen hundred have returned since the war, and these are mostly middle-aged or elderly people. West Germany's Basic Law prohibits discrimination because of religion or race. But the dreadful experience of the Jewish people under Hitler's rule is certain to prevent thousands from returning to what was once their homeland.

In the past decade student activists have made headlines on several occasions. Their demonstrations, marked at times by violence, have usually been brief. The older generation, accustomed to discipline and respect for authority, has given them little support. The German socialist student federation, the SDS, has taken a firm stand against certain political developments, voiced their opposition to the war in Vietnam, and preached about the philosophy of Mao and their distaste for American imperialism. When Kurt Kiesinger became chancellor of West Germany through a coalition of political parties in 1966, they demonstrated. When the shah of Persia visited Germany a year later they did so again.

A sociology student who was raised in East Germany gained world attention as a leader in the SDS for his opposition to the coalition that made Kiesinger chancellor and to the establishment in general. Rudi Dutschke, often called "Red Rudi," is a young activist who does not approve of violence. As a pacifist he refused to serve in the East German army and went to West Germany. His wife is an American theology student in the university in West Berlin. During demonstrations in West Berlin a young student, Benno Ohnesorg, was shot by the police. This aroused the temper of the SDS and of Rudi Dutschke. Axel Springer, publisher of many of West Germany's major newspapers and news magazines, became the target of SDS wrath because of his attacks on the student organization. This conflict reached its peak when, in 1966, a man fired several shots at Dutschke as he was leaving SDS headquarters and wounded him severely. The incident was followed by marches on the Springer editorial offices in some of the large cities in Germany.

Statistics show that the two Germanies, West and East, have progressed at about the same rate economically. But life in the East, where economic recovery and prosperity are not as obvious as in the West, is far less enjoyable. There is little variety in consumer goods and few of the luxuries that are available to citizens of the western sector are ever seen. East Germans work harder at lower wages and work well beyond the age when their western counterparts have retired to enjoy leisure time and the good life. However, in both East and West there is hope for eventual reunification even if the chances of this happening appear dim today.

# Index

# The Authors

Raymond A. Wohlrabe has spent most of his life on the Pacific coast. For many years, until his retirement in 1966, Mr. Wohlrabe taught science at the West Seattle High School in Seattle, and for part of that time was the head of the science department there. He has traveled through the Orient, the South Pacific, Central America and the Canal Zone, the West Indies, Dutch and British Guianas, Venezuela, all of Western Europe, most of Canada, and every state of the United States. One result of these travels is a long list of published books and articles. Mr. Wohlrabe also writes on scientific subjects, and in 1966 received the Washington State Governor's Award for his writing.

Now living in Vancouver, British Columbia, Werner E. Krusch grew up in Germany, lived in France for two years, and emigrated to Canada in 1951. His major hobbies are photography, travel, and sports; he is an accountant and is active in coaching soccer in the West Vancouver community program. He and Mr. Wohlrabe have traveled widely together to obtain material for their books. They have collaborated on five books in the Portraits of the Nations Series, as well as *Picture Map Geography of Western Europe* and *The Key to Vienna*.